I wish I knew all this before I st
barely any sales show that I lc
anything about being a BESTS
if no one knows my work exist
and has given me hope that ma··· ····· ·· · ··· ··· ·· ··· ···
my books out there to someone other than my immediate family.
Book Marketing Made Simple has hit the nail on the head and
Karen's wealth of experience will help so many authors or wannabe
authors see their work flourish. She offers fantastic advice that
makes perfect sense in a practical and easy to follow format. I was
hooked from page one and you will be too.

Angela De Souza, Women's Business Club and author of *I
Did it in my Pyjamas* and many other unknown books!

Book Marketing Made Simple is jam packed with great nuggets
and key steps on everything any author would want to know about
marketing their book and more! I like the fact that it is easy to dip
in and out of, so that you can read areas that particularly interest
you, and it also has some really useful timesaving strategies. The
case studies and tips show that Karen knows what she's talking
about and how she can help you. It is an all-round good read and
excellent book on every aspect to help authors to maximise their
marketing opportunities and sell more books!

Steve Preston, The Career Catalyst and author of
*Portfolio Careers – How to Work for Passion, Pleasure
and Profit, Winning Through Career Change* and *Winning
Through Redundancy*

I love this book! From start to finish, it's absolutely crammed full
of useful and inspirational advice on how to get the most out of
writing and publishing a book, written in an easy to follow, bite-size
chunk approach. And having published five books herself, Karen
Williams knows her stuff when it comes to book-aligned marketing.

This is a step-by-step guide on how to build a successful
business with a book as a core marketing strategy. It definitely
over delivers, which is a nice change from a lot of other books out
there on the same subject by authors who just use their book to
lead you into their expensive programmes. Karen's book openly

and generously shares detailed knowledge covering every aspect of creating a book that is in alignment with your business and a business that is in alignment with your book!

In addition to the tips and useful 'things to think about' summaries, Karen uses her own and her client's experiences to give useful real-life examples of strategies that have worked or not worked and this is invaluable. She even offers some useful free resources via a special website link.

Whether you are a new or experienced author, or maybe even just started out and haven't yet written a word, this book will help you align and leverage your efforts to make more impact, sell more books, help more people and ultimately grow your business. And that's something we all need.

Having published my first book with little knowledge of the industry and no real plan for its marketing other than my own raw enthusiasm, I'm delighted to have this book by my side as I prepare to launch my second, and all those that will follow. A definitive guide that will pay for itself a thousand times over.

Ellen Watts, author of *Cosmic Ordering Made Easier: how to have more of what you want more often* and *Get it Sorted – for once, for all, for GOOD*

Writing a book is only part of the challenge, selling it is another and each requires very different skills and knowledge sets. In her book, Karen clearly demonstrates the huge range of marketing opportunities that begin even before putting pen to paper. Your challenge after reading this book will no longer be how to market your book, but more, which of these great methods to choose. An invaluable practical guide to marketing your masterpiece.

Louise Wiles, Thriving Abroad and co-author of *Thriving Abroad: The Definitive Guide to International Relocation Success*

Writing a book is challenging, marketing it, even more so. Putting yourself and your book out there can be a big step outside your comfort zone for many people; it was for me! And yet why go to the bother of writing a book to build your business in order to help more people, and then do nothing with it ... Here you will gain Karen's valuable insight (and those of other experts), gaining access to some very clever ways to market your book and your business. Furthermore, there is a choice of strategies to suit your personality and preferred communication methods. As a finance coach, I have seen many businesses spend enormous amounts of money on their marketing, all on fruitless strategies. Here you will get some great strategies whilst saving a fortune too. As an author who markets her books, and discusses with other authors on what they've done, I can testify that the strategies do work. Furthermore, as an accountant I can testify to the savings too. They are all great value for money! The only thing left for you to do is choose the ones you want to do and then go do them.

Helen Monaghan, HM Coaching and author of *Successful Business Minds* and *12 Steps to Improve Your Cashflow*

I was fortunate enough to peer review the draft of this book. Having worked with Karen to get my first book published some of it was familiar. But obviously, no matter how time you spend with someone they cannot articulate all of their wisdom. This book is just packed with valuable nuggets. I found myself compelled to methodically go through step by step to ensure I had truly maximised my potential to market my book. Guess what? I hadn't. There is so much knowledge and wisdom shared in this book not only from Karen but other marketing experts that I found myself able to not only learn new things but also improve current processes. This will definitely become one of those books with the pages written all over and completely bent backwards as it will be with me every step of the way with all my future marketing activity. Thank you Karen.

Sheryl Andrews, Step by Step Listening and author of *Manage your Critic – From Overwhelm to Clarity in 7 Steps*

Karen has written a book that *works*. It is a great read, with many case studies and stories, and at the same time is a supremely practical guide to the whole process of marketing a book. Starting with the very first glimmer of your idea – through writing, promoting, funding, and publishing – with detailed guidance all the way, this book comes highly recommended.

Mary Lunnen, Dare to Blossom Life Coaching and author of *Dare to Blossom: Coaching and Creativity* and *The Dare to Blossom Rediscovery Cards Companion Guide*

Some superb hints and tips contained within the book that I will use for marketing my own book. Help to navigate the social media minefields was just what I needed, and information about Goodreads was new to me. I loved the detailed tips for the physical launch party, and the other options of a virtual launch, or an Amazon bestseller launch were intriguing options. I am already implementing the advice and reaping the rewards, thank you!

Jane Langston, The Amatsu Training School Ltd, and co-author of *Making Sense of Learning Human Anatomy and Physiology*

BOOK MARKETING MADE SIMPLE

A Practical Guide to Selling, Promoting and
Launching Your Business Building Book

KAREN WILLIAMS

Printed in the United Kingdom

First Printing, 2017

ISBN 978-0-9957390-2-4 (Print)
ISBN 978-0-9957390-3-1 (e-book)

Librotas Books
Portsmouth
Hampshire
PO2 9NT

www.LibrotasBooks.com

Contents

Foreword

I was introduced to Karen when she approached me for an interview for her first book, *The Secrets of Successful Coaches*, in 2009. I've been watching her progress ever since, and never expected her to go on and write four more books!

As the author of many books myself, having written my first book in 1994 and now authored and co-authored over 18 internationally published books, I know the challenges authors face when it comes to marketing. So I was delighted to be asked to endorse Karen's latest book.

This book includes useful information based on the lessons Karen has learned not only with her own journey as an author, but also the lessons of her many clients who have now worked with her.

It is a blend of wise words and brings together some useful ways in which authors can make the most of their words, skills and knowledge. This is an excellent offering from a seasoned professional.

Gladeana McMahon, FAC, FBACP, FIMS, FISMA, FRSA. Chair Emeritus, Association for Coaching

Acknowledgements

When I wrote my first book in 2009, I said never again, and here I am on my fifth! I could never have done this without the support of a great team, community, and readers who come back time and time again to be inspired by my books.

I'd specifically like to thank my clients for engaging me to help them to plan, write, publish and market their books, and for many of them allowing me to share their own success stories in this book.

I'd also like to thank my team: Tracy Harris my PA who keeps me on track and is my right hand woman, Sheryl Andrews who has been supporting me and our clients and helping to run our events, Rebecca Adams from European Coaching Retreats who supports the writing retreat in Spain, Louise Lubke Cuss my brilliant editor, and Samantha Pearce who has come on board in 2017 to support my clients with the design and publication of their books through the Librotas Books publishing imprint, and has also contributed an article to the book.

Thank you to Gladeana McMahon who has been part of my journey since I interviewed her for my first book in the summer of 2009 and has kindly written the foreword for this book, and also to those who reviewed my book and provided me with valuable feedback.

I am the first to say that I don't claim to know everything, and there are other experts who I'd recommend you listen to on your journey. That's why I've invited some key people to contribute with tips and advice. Thank you to Steve Bimpson (my mentor), Ginny Carter, Alison Colley, Mark Edmunds, Nicky Kriel, Suzii Fido, Louise Craigen, Naomi Johnson, Ebonie Allard, Lisa Ferland, Ellen Watts, Helen McCusker, and Dielle Hannah.

Lastly, thank you to my family and friends for putting up with me whilst I was writing this book, and for giving me the support and time to get it done!

INTRODUCTION

CHAPTER 1
Author mistakes and marketing secrets

The biggest mistake that many new business authors make is failing to promote their book at all stages of its creation.

They dedicate hours to carrying out research on their topic, looking for a unique angle and hook, creating their framework, and putting their words down on paper. Then they edit and re-edit their work to polish the final version of their manuscript.

In the meantime, they research the publishing options, either spending lots of time finding an agent or a publisher, or choosing to invest money and effort in the self-publishing or partnership route.

Their book is produced, and they feel excited when they receive their shiny new copies with their name on the cover. But it's not long before the resulting books sit in their cupboard or garage, and they fail to promote, market, or sell their masterpiece.

- They don't actually tell anyone they've written it, so nobody knows that they have!

- The book sits on Amazon with no reviews, and they wonder why it doesn't get noticed.

- They don't have a plan to use their book as a marketing and business building tool.

You too may feel that once you've got your book out there, the hard work should be over! You've probably spent a lot of time and energy writing it, and you may simply run out of steam when it's time to promote it.

You may feel fearful. Even though you've written and published your book, you may still wonder what people will think, whether they are going to like it, and how to cope with negative feedback. But if you never share your wisdom with your ideal audience, how will you ever know?

You may not have a plan to promote your book, which is an essential element if it's going to do what you wanted it to do for your business when you started!

If you want to use your book to build your credibility, stand out and raise your profile, you need to promote your book. If your big dream is to generate more income, sell lots of copies and build your business, then you need to read on. This book will give you the tools and strategies to take effective action!

Who I am and why I've written this book

Before I move on, let me tell you more about me and why I've written this book. I wrote my first book in 2009, and this book put me and my business on the map. *Book Marketing Made Simple* is now my fifth. After many of my clients – primarily coaches, therapists and consultants – saw the success that I was having with my books, and asked me to support them to write theirs, I rebranded as the Book Mentor in 2016, and Librotas was born.

I've taken many clients through the process of planning, writing, publishing and promoting books that will help them to build their business and develop their brand. After the success of my third book, *Your Book is the Hook* (www.yourbookisthehook.com), which goes through my six-step process to write, publish and promote your book, I wanted to drill down in more detail into the sixth part of the process – how to market your book.

I've had plenty of experience of marketing, with many successes and mistakes along the way. My clients are always asking me to jot down the tips that they can use to promote their own books, and I find myself repeating the same things to them again and again. Now it's time to share them with you!

This book is primarily aimed towards business owners who want to create a physical book, and may also produce an e-book and audiobook alongside this. These days it's easy to publish print on demand books (which is something I can help you with), and for many of the strategies I mention, you would benefit from having a physical book to promote, although many of the strategies can also be applied to those who are solely producing an e-book.

Your book may be a manual, textbook, how-to guide, self-help book, anthology, parable, memoir, or any type of book that you hope will be a marketing tool and credibility builder. If you don't have your business head on when you're writing, you'll find that your book will never make you money, and never reach the right people and influence them in a positive way. Many fiction writers may also benefit from some of the ideas that I share.

The strategies in this book will allow you to make the most of your hard work, knowledge and writing, and ultimately help you to grow your business through your book. You can find out more about me in the final chapter and at www.librotas.com.

My goal and your goal

My goal is to show you different ways in which you can market your book, to use it to get you noticed, and help you to become more visible. You don't have to do them all. Actually if you do them all, you'll be exhausted!

 **DETERMINE YOUR GOAL**

Before you get going, I suggest you think about what your goal is for your book. Knowing what you want to get from your book is a key factor in the activities you choose to do and what you decide to do first.

- Is it important that it's a bestseller?

- Do you want to use it to raise your credibility?

- Would you like to reach more people?

- Are you motivated by making a bigger difference in the world through sharing your expertise?

Actually, why don't you start by writing your goal down now?

_____

_____

_____

In this book, I'll give you a comprehensive selection of options that you can take, so that you can find the ones that will help you to reach your goal.

How to market your book

What many people don't realise is that marketing is actually one of the first things you need to think about when you start to write your book, whether you've taken the traditional publishing route or are self-publishing your book as an indie author. This book is designed to help you to market your book (and your business) alongside your writing. If you've picked up this book at the latter stages or after launching, you can still follow the advice in this book, but you may need to be more focused in your approach.

At whatever stage you pick up this book and follow the strategies, you need to be willing to shout about your book from the rooftops and tell everyone you know. And if you do start marketing at the early stages, then once you've published your book the marketing will be seamless. You will be able to continue implementing the strategies that already work, and you may simply be making a few tweaks to use your book to raise your profile.

You may find that you're already doing some of the marketing ideas that I suggest in this book to build your business, and please continue with these if they are working for you. With regards to the marketing activities that you wish to follow in addition to those you are doing already, it's important that you take action on the ones that work for you, that you enjoy doing, and that will help you to reach your ideal clients and readers. There's not much point in asking for speaking engagements if this scares you witless and you'll never do it. There's not much point in creating a community of people online if technology is not your thing or you're not willing to outsource it, and especially if you know you'll be sporadic at keeping in touch with people. But sometimes you do need to stretch yourself to do the things that scare you, so don't use this as an excuse!

It's up to you to pick the things that you know deep down will help you. These need to be the things that you want to do, and will do religiously and regularly to get you and your book noticed. You'll probably start with a handful of strategies, but as you develop your business and your books, I hope you'll integrate, streamline and automate your marketing, which will make it simpler to implement. I'll show you how I do it for my business and books.

In time, your marketing focus may change, as you may well outsource some of the strategies that you do yourself in the beginning, allowing you to do what you're best at – which is probably reflected in the topic of your book!

I advise that you take a multi-pronged approach. Having a mixture of offline and online strategies that you do consistently at all stages of your book's launch is likely to give you the most effective results. Just be consistent with your marketing, measure your results, tweak your activities, and then you will be able to get an effective return from the investment in your book. Many of these – as you'll see when you make your way through this book – will be from products, services, and other back-end products that you sell off the back of your book.

How to read this book

If you're wondering where to start, I've broken this book down into three main sections.

Before moving to the first main section, I'll give you an introduction to what you need in place before you start to market your book, and ideally before you start to write it!

I'll also tell you how and when you need to market your book. I'll show you some of the key strategies I'll be mentioning in this book before breaking them down into three key areas:

Pre-launch – this is when you're in the starting phase of writing your book, up until the time you launch it. As I mentioned earlier, you may be doing some of the things I suggest already in your business, and others might be things that you've thought of doing, but haven't been sure where to start. You'll probably find that you will continue to use many of the suggestions as part of your ongoing business marketing, as well as to promote your book.

Launch – I'll be showing you specific things that you can do to launch your book, some of which need some planning, so please don't wait until your actual launch date to make these happen. These include things like promoting your book on Amazon, having a launch party, and getting publicity from your book.

Post-launch – It's really important to keep the momentum going once you've published, and many people fail to recognise that you need to continually promote your book. I'll be giving you some strategies so that you continue to tell people about your book and how it can help them.

If you're in the early stages of writing your book, then I suggest you read the whole of this book now. You will learn about some of the things you need to do later, even if you dip back in at the stage when you need to re-read the information. If you're further down the road, read the book anyway, as there are things that you can do at all stages and integrate together when you're ready.

What's next?

Whatever book you're writing to build your credibility, it's vital that you write your best book. Sharing your most impressive secrets and strategies is a sure way to achieve greater success. And marketing your book effectively will give you the best results!

I'll be sharing some of my own secrets and strategies that I use, so that you can put the ideas into practice without it taking up much of your time, and ideally you'll be able to use some of the content from the book you're writing. You'll also get advice from other experts and case studies from my clients to inspire you. You'll find that I will occasionally reference additional resources that you can find on my website, as I can only fit so much into this book! Feel free to download them as they'll support the information you'll get from reading this book.

One last thing: I know that you'll get some great strategies from this book, and if you'd like my team and me to give you personal support at any stage of the book process – from planning to writing, publishing AND marketing your book, then please pop over to www.librotas.com to find out how, or email karen@librotas.com.

Let's get started!

CHAPTER 2
Marketing must-knows

When someone asks you about your book, what do you say?

Are you clear who it is for, what its purpose is, and how it can help people?

Or are you more inclined to mutter about writing it and perhaps end up failing to shine?

When you've spent days, weeks, and months crafting your book, it makes sense to market it effectively. But there are some things you need to consider before you get stuck in and ideally before you start to write your book!

- Tell people in your community you're writing your book from the day you start to write it, as this will help to raise your profile.

- Get clear about who your book is for and your book's content, so that you'll be able to talk about it confidently.

- When you're clear on your message, you can develop your website content, blogs and other online marketing to complement this and build your personal brand.

- When you know what you're writing, you can create a good plan, stick to the point in the book, and write it easily.

- If you're pitching your book to a publisher, this will help you to write your synopsis and prepare your proposal.

- It will also help you to write the back cover for your book and approach influential people for your foreword, reviews, and testimonials.

In this chapter I want to help you to get clear on your book, who it's for, what your message is, why your story is important, and how you can create your perfect pitch.

Alignment and leverage

When I start working with my clients, alignment and leverage are my two favourite words. *Aligning* everything that you do in your business (by being clear on what you do and who you do it for) will allow you to *leverage* your knowledge through your book (allowing you to multiply the outcome of your efforts without a corresponding increase in resources).

Writing a book for your business isn't about writing any old book, it's about writing the right one for your target audience, i.e. the people who you are already working with in your business. Your ideal reader will usually be your ideal client. There's really not much point in writing a book about a different topic to a different audience, unless you're going to diversify your business or start working with a new type of client. If you're not 100% sure on this right now, you, like many of my clients, may find that the act of writing your book helps you to get clearer on who you love to work with, and your message will develop as you pull together your content.

Once you've got everything aligned, then it's important to think about leverage. How are you going to leverage your expertise? Of course your book will ideally position you as an expert, but when you start developing your content, start with the end in mind. As well as writing your book, consider what else your clients will want from you in terms of products, services, and perhaps other books?! I'll be covering all of this, but want to introduce it at this early stage so you can start thinking about it!

Your market, message and media

So let's get stuck in with the alignment part.

Many people are far too general about their content when they write their book. The most successful business building books are those which are targeted towards a particular group of people. When I mention success at this stage, I mean that your book will be successful in reaching more potential clients, creating new opportunities, and building your business – or however you define success!

That's why before you write your book or do any type of marketing you must know your ideal reader, why they should buy it, and clarify your message. In addition, for your book to stand out, it needs to be different from everything else that has been written on your topic. So do your research before you get started!

If you don't nail these things before you write and market your book, then you may well waste your time and energy. You'll struggle to bring together your book, let alone sell it and use it as a business building tool.

If you've already marketed a product, you may have heard of the 'Market, Message and Media (medium)' model.

• Your market is who your book is for, i.e. your ideal reader and client.

• Your message is about what you say that grabs their attention specifically.

• Media or medium is how you get your message to them, e.g. your marketing activities.

I'll cover the first two in this chapter to set the scene, and media will be covered throughout the book. Although if you are already totally clear on who your book is for and why they need to read it, feel free to skip the next two sections.

Your market

Who is the ideal reader for your book?

If you believe that your book will help anyone with anything, or your answer to my question is fairly vague, then I suggest you revisit this before you finish writing your book (and ideally before you start it). You will need to nail this because it is fundamentally relevant to your book and the way you market it.

Your book is your chance to position yourself as an expert, and use it as an effective marketing tool, so you may choose to niche quite deeply in your book. For example, *Book Marketing Made Simple* will only attract a limited part of the entire population, but it will help business authors who want to make money from their book, and use it as a business building strategy. And it's amazing how many business people actually want to do this!

If you're not yet clear on who your ideal reader and client is, then I suggest you do this exercise below, which is one of the things I do with many of my clients. Ultimately you want to create a book – and a business – that allows you to play to your strengths and hit your sweet spot. This is the place where you can do what you love, do what you're good at, and ideally get paid well!

CREATE YOUR CLIENT (AND READER) AVATAR

Who is your ideal reader and client?

_____

_____

_____

What is their gender?

_____

What is their age?

_____

What do they do?

_____

What is their family situation?

_____

What is their work status and income?

_____

What else differentiates them from the rest of the population?

_____

_____

What's important to them?

_____

_____

What are their goals and aspirations?

_____

_____

What are the top three problems or challenges that they need help with to achieve their goals and aspirations?

1. _____

_____

2. _____

_____

3. _____

_____

How can you solve their most pressing problems in your book?

_____

_____

_____

When you've completed your avatar, it will help you to answer questions like:

- Which magazines do they read?

- Which radio stations do they listen to?

- What do they do with their spare time?

- What are their favoured social media platforms?

- How can you reach them through your book?

Your message

Knowing your ideal reader will help you to get clear about what they want to hear from you. This makes it easier to define the topic for your book, write the content, and plan your marketing. Oh, and develop your message!

Your message may be the problem you're solving in your book or it may be new information that you're providing to your reader – or both! One caveat that I'd like to add here is this: Don't include everything you know in your book. Stick to a topic. If you've got multiple topics that you want to share, it may be that your first book gives an overview, or there may be multiple books that you need to write!

If you haven't got this far yet and you're struggling to work out your exact message, then one way that you can do this is by asking your clients and prospects to complete a survey. Although some survey tools cost money, many are free if you use a limited number of questions and are willing to analyse the data yourself.

When you carry out a survey, use a mixture of questions. You can get statistics and data by using quantitative questions, where people tick a box. You can discover your clients' language by using qualitative questions alongside these, where they share their opinions or thoughts.

Ask questions about your prospective readers' biggest challenges, ask them what they'd like instead, and get their feedback about what they'd want to find out from your book. Many of my clients have used this method, and here's a really great example.

CASE STUDY
Lorraine Palmer
author of *Raw Food in a Flash*

When Lorraine came to me to get help to write her book, she was using her book to niche in a smaller market than she was working in already. Although she worked in the raw food sphere, she wanted to use her book to position herself as the go-to person supporting ladies going through the menopause through the medium of eating a diet consisting of mainly raw food.

One of the reasons why she decided to niche in this area was that she had gone through early menopause herself, and raw food was the thing that helped her to get through it. She wanted to use these experiences to help others.

Due to the fact that Lorraine was using her book to reposition herself as an expert in a niched area, I suggested she carry out a survey as part of the research for her book.

She used Surveymonkey.com to carry out a survey to find out what people were struggling with and where they needed support.

This survey resulted in over 100 people who couldn't wait to receive her book. With their permission, Lorraine added these ladies to her mailing list so that she could keep in touch with them as she was writing it.

If you'd like to carry out a survey for your book, you can download my 'How-to guide' at www.librotas.com/free. You may also find it useful to take people in your target readership out for coffee or interview them to find out what they want to hear from you in your book.

When you become clearer on your message, this will be the consistent communication that you give when you introduce yourself at networking events. It will define the content that you put on your website, and it will probably inform the marketing for your book too.

Your angle and hook

With regards to your message, it's important not to have a message that's the same as everyone else's – as there may be a million other things written on your topic – so think about your unique angle and hook. This is a concept that I introduced in my third book, *Your Book is the Hook*. Your angle is your take on a subject and your hook is the thing that grabs people's attention.

Your angle might be the type of person you are writing for; perhaps you have a specific group of people in mind who are your ideal readers. Your hook might be the problem you are solving for these individuals. The thing that makes your book different may be the unique way in which you address this problem and provide a solution.

Linked closely to your message is what you want to get known for. This is one of the things I'm always asking new clients. If you want to get known as the go-to person in your industry, it helps if you know what this is and get this across in your book! Let me give you another client example.

CASE STUDY
Jenny Phillips
author of *Eat to OUTSMART Cancer*

Jenny Phillips published her first book, *Eat to OUTSMART Cancer*, in 2015. I helped her to write the book and develop her message. The motivation behind Jenny's business as a nutritionist was that she went into this profession after using nutrition in her own bid to overcome breast cancer when she was 39.

After many years practising as a nutritionist, she found that she worked with many patients who were going through a similar experience, or wanted to improve their health to avoid cancer.

With each patient she saw, she found she was saying the same thing. That's why she wrote her book: to get this message to more people who needed to hear it.

The angle that she took was having her book specifically aimed towards those going through cancer and those who wished to avoid the disease.

Her hook was the positive results that she and her clients were getting from following her programme.

This helped her to raise her profile, and while she was writing her book, Jenny was approached to run nutrition events for a cancer charity, and that was before she'd even finished and published it!

Your story

The topic and the content for your book may well stem from your story, how this has impacted on the person you are today, and what you're saying in your book. You've already heard from two of my clients: Jenny, whose experience of breast cancer literally changed her life path, and Lorraine who changed the course of her business after going through an early menopause. For both of these ladies, their experiences have impacted on the books that they have written and the niche market that they support.

Get clear on why you're the best person to write this book. Become clear on how your knowledge and expertise makes you an expert. Be aware of how your journey has led you to where you are today. All of these will help you to write your book with authenticity and vulnerability. Also be willing to share your story in your book, as this will inspire and help your readers.

From my experience it isn't always easy, and you may well have to dig deep and be brave to tell people about your journey. Here's another example from a client.

CASE STUDY
Rochelle Bugg
author of *Help! My Mum's Got Cancer*

In 2012, Rochelle Bugg nursed her mum, who had a brain tumour, and blogged about the experience. As a carer in her twenties, there wasn't much support available for her and her two sisters, and her dad had sadly passed away ten years earlier. She wrote her blog to keep her sane, share her thoughts, and help others in a similar situation.

To reach more people and make a bigger difference, in 2016 she decided to turn her blog into a book. She wants to help people through her story and her journey, and ensure that other people don't have to go through the same tough times. She wants to inspire other young carers and give them the tools that she didn't have when she needed them.

Although at the time of writing she hasn't yet published her book, she told me how it has helped her to date:

"The book so far has helped me to get clear on the value of what I have to offer. This clarity has enabled me to work out what my business will look like going forward.

"I've found that writing a book is a great resource when it comes to social media content. I think it's important to remember what a rich source of 'readymade' content a book gives you. You can pick out quotes to make into memes but also have themes that you can pick for longer posts and newsletter content. For example, I've tweaked content from my book as the basis to write articles for big international lifestyle websites. The content that you write in your book is really versatile and can be repackaged in so many ways – articles for third parties, speaking engagements, and a framework for an e-course.

"I think there's a certain kudos and automatic respect that comes from having written a book on a specific subject. It's great at helping to establish yourself within an industry and sets you apart from the competition. Even being able to write a press release and quote yourself as 'published author of book XYZ' is so much stronger and more likely to be picked up.

"The book writing process has also helped to build my confidence – it's reassured me that I have a body of knowledge and experience to share, as well as helping me get clear on my areas of expertise. In turn that will help with marketing when writing press releases, pitching stories to media, and seeking out speaking engagements, as I'm a lot clearer on who I am and my message."

I'm sure that you can see how Rochelle's story and hook has already helped her to build her business through her book before she's actually published it. Most importantly it will help her to reach those who need her support.

Rochelle's book is written in a memoir style. She is chronologically taking people through her journey, and this can be an easier way to share your story. I also did this for my fourth book, *The Mouse That Roars*. But when you are drip feeding your story into your book in a how-to guide like this, it's trickier. Hopefully you will see some of the ways in which I've done this, as well as sharing some of my clients' stories. I've touched on this a little more with information about the different types of books you could write in chapter 6 of *Your Book is the Hook* (www.yourbookisthehook.com).

Your perfect pitch

Lastly in this chapter, just like you'd have an elevator pitch for your business, it also helps to have a great pitch for your book. This will help you with some of the examples I gave at the beginning of the chapter, and if you've made some notes, you'll be ready to put it into place.

If someone asked you to give a short précis on your book in 30 seconds or less, what would you say?

CREATING YOUR PERFECT PITCH

You might find answering the questions below will give you a good starting point.

Who specifically is your book for?

_____

What problems are your ideal readers facing?

_____

What fresh, new or innovative insights does your book bring?

_____

What is your message?

_____

What is your angle?

_____

What is your hook?

_____

How will you grab your reader's attention with your message?

_____

What makes your book different from anything else written on your topic?

_____

Why are you the best person to write this book?

_____

How does your story and journey impact on your book?

_____

The answers to these questions will not only help you to write your book, but they'll also give you ideas that will help you to promote and sell your book before you've actually finished it.

 **THINGS TO THINK ABOUT**

Get clear on your message before you start to write your book to ensure that you are meeting the needs of your clients and what they want to know.

Know your angle and hook. What makes your book different from other things that have already been written on your topic?

If you're using your book to reposition yourself in a specific niche, get clear on what your ideal readers want to hear from you.

You may well be writing your book because of your own experiences and story. Get clear on this story as you write and develop your book.

_____

_____

_____

_____

_____

_____

_____

_____

CHAPTER 3
When and how to get started

I've already mentioned that it's important that you start to market your book from the day you decide to write it. Although it may feel counterintuitive because you've got to get your book written, it will help to get you and your book noticed. If you wait until your book is published, it will take longer to create a buzz, build momentum and nurture a group of people who can't wait to get their hands on a copy.

Actually it makes sense to include your book (or books!) as part of your bigger business plan and vision, as your book is one of the tools that you have to offer your client.

Think about where your ideal readers are coming from, how you will build your community, and your sales funnel, which refers to the buying process that leads your prospective clients through various steps. This means that you are clear about where you're going to take your readers next. Perhaps you have a product that complements the book, like a workbook, audio programme, webinar series, workshop or event, and just knowing how this all fits into your sales funnel will help you with your book marketing.

Before I go into this in more detail, here are some of the strategies that most successful business authors will have in place from the day that they decide to write their book. I'll also expand on these in future chapters.

A website with the right focus

Once you know your message, it will help you with all aspects of your marketing, and one of these is a website with the right focus that supports your book. If there is a mismatch in terms of the focus and wording, then people may struggle to understand what you're writing about and who it's for. You may also decide to have an author's website where the sole purpose is to promote your book.

Your website is something that can be developed alongside writing the book, and needs to be a priority. Ideally you'll be writing the book that supports your business growth, but if you're using your book to position yourself in a new market, then you may choose to have two separate websites initially whilst making the transition.

A lead magnet and opt-in

As well as having a congruent message on your website, it's essential that you think about your reader's journey from the start.

Having a lead magnet (also known as an ethical bribe or freebie), that is the precursor to the book, will help you to develop a community of people who are interested in your book. Regularly communicating through an email newsletter with a consistent message will help them to get to know what you do and what you stand for.

One of the things that I suggest to my clients is repurposing their content. When you have a blog, video blog or podcast — more in the next point — as part of your online marketing, you can easily repurpose your information. You can turn it into a newsletter or article, rather than reinventing the wheel and continually producing new content.

Blogs, vlogs (video blogs) or podcasts

Your online presence is important. Sharing your book writing journey is a great way to get people involved from the day you pick up your pen, put your hand to your keyboard, or start speaking into your smartphone.

Revealing snippets of the book will help you to get people's feedback on your work, and creating videos or podcasts is particularly good if writing a blog feels all too much alongside your book production.

Social media presence

Having a social media presence <u>and</u> being active on social media is essential. It's not enough to have a Twitter profile and 16 followers, posting once a month. Making this part of your marketing strategy is part of the process, especially if your ideal readers use social media.

Your social media presence is equally important – if not more so – when you're hoping to be published in the traditional way. Having a large community of followers is often one of the first things that any good publisher will look for before they agree to publish your work. You'll need to have many thousands of engaged followers who want to hear what you have to say, and are ready to buy your book.

A tribe of people who love what you do

Although having a strong social media presence is important, having a tribe of people who you connect with regularly is essential. I touched on this briefly with the lead magnet, but it's not enough to just have a good lead magnet and email list. It's important to build a strong relationship with those who are in your readership, and share great content with them.

A community of people who will support you

It's important to remember that before the age of the internet, people also sold books. The best way of doing this is by having a community of people who will support you.

As well as having a business coach or book mentor, you may have a network of contacts who could contribute to the book, and promote and share it with their networks. Go networking, take your contacts for coffee, and get away from your desk! Speak at events, attend exhibitions and create joint ventures.

When you talk about your book at any stage to the right people, it will help you to meet more people interested in the end result. And this will help you to reach more people with your book.

PR message and story

I mentioned briefly in the last chapter that many authors write their book due to their experiences, knowledge or story. If you're looking to get great publicity from your book, i.e. get into the national newspapers or glossy magazines, you need to start to get clear on your story now and why you do what you do.

To make it easy to quickly respond to publicity requests, I suggest you design a short and longer biography that you can share. You'll need this also if you speak at an event, are interviewed for a podcast, or guest blog for another publication.

Are you ready to get started?

These are some ideas for starters. Over the coming sections and chapters, I will go into each of these in more detail when it's relevant. I'll also share the different things you can do at each stage of your book's launch and how you can keep your promotion going even after you've been published.

Measure your success

One last thing before we get stuck in. However you decide to market your book, don't try and do everything at once. Choose the things that work for your ideal readership, and do them consistently rather than taking a scattergun approach. And as I mentioned in chapter 1, make sure you test and measure your results.

- You may wish to think about how many books you need to sell to make your initial return on investment if you've self-published.

- If you do any form of advertising, what's your return on the money you have paid out?

- How many people do you need to have a conversation with to attain a new client?

- How many people read your newsletter or blog each week?

Work out what you want to measure, and regularly do it! Then you can make tweaks if you need to do so.

 **THINGS TO THINK ABOUT**

Market your book from the day you start to write it. Tell people about it, do your research, and get feedback on your work.

Ensure you're writing the right book — the one that will support and build your business. If you have multiple ideas, get clear on which one will make the biggest difference right now, and keep your other ideas on the backburner for later!

Make sure your book is part of your bigger vision for your business, so that you know how it fits into your existing marketing and business growth.

Review the different ways to market your book so that you can choose the best and most enjoyable ways to reach your clients. Also test and measure your results.

_____

_____

_____

_____

_____

_____

_____

SECTION 1
Pre-launch book marketing strategies

In the pre-launch stage, I want to give you strategies to make your marketing simple, so that you can use your book to market your business, and use your business to market your book. You're probably still writing and editing your book and also working with clients, and may not have a huge amount of time to focus on specific book marketing strategies.

The tips in this section are designed to get you ready for the marketing side of your book, and you'll probably use them throughout the whole process of writing and publishing it, and promoting your business. That's why I suggest that you chose the best ones for you, and be consistent with their application. Please don't try and do them all, as you'll never have time for anything else!

You may already be doing some of the things I'm talking about – like blogging, podcasts or videos – but you'll probably tweak your message slightly as you develop the information you're sharing through your book. You may also decide to do new things that you've never done before. The key to finding the right way to market your book is to intimately get to know your ideal reader, which I've touched on already, where you can find them, and how you can reach them easily.

Ultimately if you're already doing things that work, carry on with them. And if you find that new things work, then please use them to leverage your expertise.

CHAPTER 4
Work on your website and leverage your leads

One of the problems that some people face when they decide to write a book is that their website becomes outdated. When they do the research for their book, they get clearer about what they actually do, and this changes their message. This may result in tweaks to their business direction alongside writing their book, and will also require them to work on their website copy.

There may be others who are also writing a book to establish themselves in a new niche, and this will often result in a new website altogether.

That's why I'd like to start by suggesting that you review your website and what it says about you. Even if you don't fall into either category above, you may find tips in this chapter that will help you to get more leads and more traffic. You may also choose to have an author's website solely for your book that will help you to create your author platform and sell your book (I'll go into this in more detail later).

Ultimately it's important that your message is congruent if you mention your website address in your book, or if people search for you on the internet.

YOUR WEBSITE MESSAGE

Check out the home page of your website now. Does it reflect what you're talking about in your book?

Is it focused on your ideal reader and client?

_____

Is it congruent with your book's message?

_____

Does it grab your reader's attention from the moment they arrive on your page?

_____

Does it tell people about your journey, your story and why you do what you do?

_____

I help many of my clients to hone their website copy alongside supporting them with their book. Here's a great example.

CASE STUDY
Fiona Chapman
author of *The ChapWell Method: The 7 Keys to Your Success, Happiness and Wellbeing*

Fiona approached me to help her with her book. Although she already had a website when I became her book mentor in 2015, she knew that it could be improved.

I recommended a contact who supported her to develop her website whilst we worked on the copy. Fiona also developed a lead magnet to build her community at the same time as promoting her new book. The website designer helped her to implement the email marketing software to make this easier for her.

She initially chose to enable people to download a chapter from her book, which was a simple way of growing her community as well as promoting her book.

If, like Fiona, you don't already have a list in place before you start to write your book, you can develop it at the same time.

Your website won't help you unless it markets your expertise well. Although it's important that your website looks good, it needs to be functional in terms of marketing your business and your book. There's not much point in having a website that looks pretty if it doesn't actually sell you effectively.

Refreshing your website is another expense, but if you spend your precious time learning how to do the technical bits yourself, then you'll never actually get around to writing your book. My advice is that if someone else can do something better than you, outsource it, especially if they can do it quicker and cost effectively, and you can earn more money in your area of expertise.

Choosing the right web designer is important. If you have a choice between different types of website, I prefer WordPress, because my team and I can update the content. Then I only need support from my web designer when changes are more complicated.

When deciding to use your website as a marketing tool, you'll find that you get conflicting advice. Some people believe that a one page website is all you need, some will tell you to have a video only, and others will stick to the traditional ways of marketing. Whichever advice you choose to follow, it's important to note these points:

- You've only got a few seconds to capture someone's attention when they arrive on your website from a link or a search engine.

- Being different is great, as long as your message is consistent and unique.

- You need to talk about your ideal reader and what they want – it's not all about you!

One of the things that I was taught many years ago is AIDA, and this may help you to write copy for your website, blog, videos and other marketing.

The AIDA model is credited to Elias St Elmo Lewis in 1898, and it is a model that has been used for a long time. I still believe that it's useful in the twenty-first century, although there have been many adaptations to this strategy over the years.

AIDA stands for:

Attention
Interest
Desire
Action

Attention means that whatever you're producing must grab people's attention, either with an image or a great headline, or anything else that'll make them stop and look twice at it. This might include asking a question, giving a teaser, using a story, having a compelling video on your home page, or saying something controversial.

Interest means that what you write or show is interesting from the reader's viewpoint. This includes talking about benefits rather than features, keeping your content simple, and perhaps having statistics that prove something.

Desire means that your reader feels a growing desire to feel the way you're making him or her feel through your words or images, and your message meets their needs and wants. This may include techniques like scarcity (this might be a time-limited special offer for your book), and social proof like case studies or testimonials which endorse your message.

Action. If AID doesn't result in any action, then nothing will happen, and all the AID will just go to waste. Ensure that every piece of marketing material you produce tells your reader what they must do next.

Your website doesn't have to be overly complicated; actually I believe that less is more. If you're creating a new website, the most important things are having a lead magnet to grow your community, and you may also wish to have an 'About you' page (ideally with a professional photograph), details of your products and services, a contact page so people can get in touch with you, and a blog if this is one of the ways you decide to market your business.

It's also important that your website is found and here are some tips from Steve Bimpson to help you to do this. I'll also be expanding on some of the things he mentions in subsequent chapters.

 FIVE ESSENTIAL STEPS TO GET YOUR WEBSITE FOUND BY STEVE BIMPSON

You have a website. You've listened to a lot of the advice you've been given, and:

- You've spent money on a web designer and your website looks professional.

- You've made sure that your content is targeted, squarely, at your ideal client.

- Your content is all about your ideal client and his/her problems. It's focused on them, from their perspective, not on you from your perspective.

- You've considered your customer journey – the process that your typical ideal client goes through before they buy – and your website has been designed to take them on that journey.

- You've got lead magnets, opt-in forms and different means to encourage enquiries from visitors.

- You have a well thought through follow-up process in place and ready to go.

Despite all of this, you're not happy. The problem is your website still isn't working for you, because people aren't finding it! So, what should you do?

eve there are five essential steps that you need to take if you want the right people (your ideal clients) to find your website at the right time, i.e. when they have a problem.

Step 1 – Create a web strategy

Sadly, most websites are built and, once finished, are never touched again until the next time they get overhauled – which can be years.

A website is a dynamic marketing tool and to really work for you it should be used that way. It should be developed as you and your business grow. That requires an ongoing strategy that should be decided from the start. Then you can plan the content to deliver that strategy and decide when you're going to add it to your website.

Step 2 – Do your research

There are a number of tools that can help you identify what questions your ideal clients are asking when they search online.

These include Google's Keyword Planner, Google Trends, SEO Book, and Word Tracker to name a few.

You need to find out what keywords and phrases your ideal clients are searching for online, how often these words and phrases get searched, and how competitive they are.

These results feed into your overall strategy – the idea being to create a specific blog post that, effectively, 'answers' each individual question.

Step 3 – Tell the search engines what every page is about

Most people don't bother with Search Engine Optimisation (SEO), but you need to ensure that search engines know, precisely, what the content of any specific post or page is about. If the search engines don't know, how can they send you your ideal clients?

Step 4 – Make sure everything's 'joined up'

You may be familiar with Stephen R Covey's book, *The 7 Habits of Highly Effective People*. Habit number two is 'Always begin with the end in mind'.

Consider this with every individual piece of content on your website and ensure that you make it clear to your visitors what they need to do to get there. If you don't, they won't!

Step 5 – Create a social media strategy

A lot of people post things on their social media and, although this step does include sharing your content, there's an important step in strategy that many people forget. That is the need to actually *build* your social media following.

I see a lot of businesses which continuously share their content to what is a fairly insignificant number of followers that are poorly targeted. Unless you have an ongoing strategy to build your social media following, the chances are your activity and content is unlikely to do you much good.

Something to remember

It's important to focus your efforts in the right way and in the right direction. Too many people get hung up with numbers.

They think that more visitors and more followers is what it's all about. That isn't true.

What's important is that your visitors are highly targeted. You should be attracting your ideal clients because they're the ones that are going to find value in your website when they visit.

If you focus on numbers, what tends to happen is the targeting becomes far less focused and you end up in a situation that I've often come across: one where a website has a lot of visitors but they still don't get many enquiries – usually because the visitors aren't their ideal clients and, therefore, aren't interested in making an enquiry.

Steve Bimpson, supporting, nurturing and inspiring business owners to achieve extraordinary results at www.justthinkbig.co.

Create a lead magnet and email opt-in

Capturing your ideal client's attention on your website isn't just about having some nice to read copy; you want people to do something, like I mentioned in the call to action above. If you'd like to build a community of people who want to buy your book, you need to focus on building your mailing list. You'll have a sign-up box on your website where people leave their name and email address in return for receiving something valuable (the lead magnet I mentioned earlier). This will link to mailing software – like MailChimp, AWeber or Infusionsoft – which will, once set up, automatically deliver this freebie and allow you to connect with people who are interested in what you have to say.

You can communicate with your community regularly via email and (of course) tell them about your book! Although you might think that implementing an email system is expensive, think about how much time it would take if you were constantly collating spreadsheets and sending out individual emails!

It also means that when people come onto your website, they do something. They are more likely to leave their contact details, rather than wander off to another website to do something else. With this in mind, I'd suggest you have one (or all) of the following:

- A squeeze or lead page for your lead magnet, where all you want people to do is sign up for your lead magnet (AIDA would typically apply when writing the copy for this option). I use the Squeeze Page Toolkit, which I mention further in chapter 11.

- A sign-up box on the right hand side or towards the top of your website, so that people can see it at a glance, but you do need to sell the benefits of signing up.

- You may choose to have your sign-up box 'pop up' after someone has been on your website for a designated amount of time. This is one of the features of Squeeze Page Toolkit, and some other systems allow you to do the same.

Your lead magnet needs to have a catchy title. One of my best performing lead magnets was called 'Why you can't make money as a life coach'. Your title may be 'away from' in its message like I did for this option, or 'towards' in terms of telling people positively what they'll get from signing up.

If you do have a free offering already in place, I'd advise you to check that it is the right one. Typically a PDF, report, checklist, e-book, video series, audio series or e-course, it needs to be something easy to consume. When you are using it to market your book, ideally it is the precursor to your book, and then your book is the next stage.

Although your lead magnet needs to look professional, a simple PDF may be all you need at the starting point to help you to build your list. If you are in the latter stages of writing your book, another option would be to give away a chapter of your book, like Fiona Chapman did, as this will raise interest in your message – as long as you promote it.

I also suggest you write a series of autoresponders that allow you to keep in touch with people when they sign up. These are a pre-programmed series of emails that you can set up. These will be delivered automatically by your email provider once people have registered for your lead magnet. This will add extra value for your new subscribers and tell them more about what you do.

Let me give you an example. When I launched *Your Book is the Hook*, I developed a 'How to write a book' checklist which you can download from my website at www.librotas.com/checklist. To align it with *Your Book is the Hook*, I asked my graphic illustrator to design it for me. Over the last couple of years, it's had some great feedback in terms of the presentation, what I've included, and how it's delivered. It is simply a two page document that takes subscribers through the six-step process of writing a book that I talk about in *Your Book is the Hook*. I have added value by having a series of autoresponders that give a summary of each step, taking people through each section of the book (and checklist) to give more information about the process and why each step is important.

In addition I send regular informative emails, useful information, and share my blog posts with my mailing list. I also promote my books and programmes and make occasional offers. You may well be on my list already and I hope this shows you how I use this system to build relationships and develop my community.

Although in many industries newsletter 'open rates' (the number of people who open marketing emails) have dropped, and sign-ups are less common than they used to be, it is still a model that works. It's something I've done since I started out in 2006, although my lead magnets have certainly evolved over the years. It worked for me successfully before and after I wrote and published my books.

It is something that I suggest my clients do – and I suggest you do it too!

My client, Helen Monaghan, has another great example of how she did it. When she started working with me on a one-to-one basis, she had a plan to write one book and went on to write two!

CASE STUDY
Helen Monaghan
author of *Successful Business Minds* and *12 Steps to Improve Your Cashflow*

Helen employed me as her book mentor in the summer of 2015. Within ten months, she'd written not one but two books. The first one was a short e-book *12 Steps to Improve Your Cashflow* (but it was still an impressive 10,000 words!).

The e-book served two purposes. It was the perfect download on her website where people could leave their name and email address to get a PDF copy of the book. She also uploaded it to Amazon and people could pay £1.99 if they preferred to buy it on Kindle rather than leave their contact details.

Helen's main goal for this e-book was to build her community, which she did very impressively. She shares regular content with her subscribers, has talked about her journey of writing her books, and has also promoted her products and programmes.

Both books have helped her to build a following, fill her book launch, and sell her book *Successful Business Minds* once it was published. Both books have helped her to raise her profile, attract more clients, and collaborate with other coaches and accountants.

Since launching these books, Helen has been working alongside me on her next books and products. Her books have already allowed her to develop products and events which are helping her to build her business, which I'll talk about next.

Create your product funnel

The earlier you build your community, tribe, and list of raving fans, the easier it will be to sell your book and build your business.

As well as putting your lead magnet into place, it's important to think about the next steps for your readers. Once people have read your book, what do you want them to do next?

You may go into more detail on a particular topic in a product or programme, or give your readers access to you personally, so that you can support them further.

Although the products and services that you decide to offer will depend on the type of book that you've written, it is important to have these in place if you want to build multiple streams of income alongside your book.

Most people will have a lead magnet, the book, and then a low cost product that they sell via their website. This is normally a digital product, which means that once it has been created it needs little or none of your actual time to deliver to your clients.

Next you may have something that is higher in cost, which you also may deliver one to many, such as a membership programme, workshop or event, or a higher value online product, before offering your one-to-one or VIP services. Although I'll go into more detail of specifics and examples in chapter 20, it's worth being aware of this at the pre-launch stage of your book.

I suggest that you fill in the box below with the products and services you offer already and make a note of those which you need to develop later.

WHAT PRODUCTS OR SERVICES DO YOU HAVE OR NEED TO DEVELOP?

Lead magnet _____

_____

Book _____

_____

Low cost product (usually up to £100) _____

_____

Medium cost product (usually between £100–£500) _____

_____

Higher cost 1-1 service _____

_____

VIP service _____

_____

Once you have different products and services available for different people, this will help you to offer the right thing to the right person. There will be some clients who only want exclusive access to you, and others who won't be able or ready to invest in your one-to-one services and may prefer a group programme. Although I do suggest that you find out what people want from you before you design a product that nobody wants to buy.

You don't, however, have to have all of these in place at the beginning. If you don't yet have a product, then I'd suggest you either create a complementary programme alongside writing your book and develop your existing content further, or promote your one-to-one services instead. Working with clients will give you great content for your book (and probably some great case studies). You'll also get to know what people want from you later as you work on your book. I'll go into more detail in chapter 20.

If you're going to sell your books, products and programmes, you need to have a good website and a community of people who love what you do. Then when you develop the relationship with your tribe through great content and regular communication, you'll have people who get value from what you do and some will want more of what you have to offer. I'll focus on this in the upcoming chapters.

 **THINGS TO THINK ABOUT**

Ensure that your website and message is clearly aimed towards your ideal client and reader.

Building your community and list needs to be a priority alongside writing your book. Keeping in touch with them regularly is essential.

Think about your reader's journey including the first step before your book, and the next steps after they've read your book.

Different levels of product will give your clients different ways they can access you and your services, and will allow you to generate multiple streams of income in your business.

_____

_____

_____

_____

_____

_____

_____

_____

CHAPTER 5
Build on your blog

You might be thinking 'Karen I've got to write my book, how on earth am I going to have time to do all of this marketing stuff at the same time?' Well can I let you into a couple of secrets?

You don't have to do everything at once! Although I must warn you that if you *just* focus on the marketing side, and *never* take the time to write, you'll *never* actually have a book to market!

It is a fine line between spending time on the marketing side of your book, and spending time actually writing it. There are also some shortcuts that you can take to make life easier whilst you prioritise your time.

Blogging is a great way to grow a community of people who want to read your book; it's free and only requires your time once your blog is set up. In effect you're writing short articles which you publish on your website. These can be used to help your readers and showcase how you can support them.

Here are some advantages of blogging:

- Internet search engines love new content and having regular blogs and updates will help drive traffic to your website, thus enabling your prospective clients and readers to find you online.

- When you write compelling content, people will become interested in what you say, and how it relates to them.

- It gives you the chance to stand out and build your credibility and authority before you've actually been published.

- When you have an effective strategy, you can connect with your audience by providing regular good content that answers their questions and problems.

- You can promote your services by writing relevant articles that relate to your next promotion.

- With a good call to action, you can generate more leads and subscribers to your mailing list.

If you choose to blog, I believe that it's important to be consistent in terms of how often you post a new article, but it doesn't have to be difficult. All of the strategies in this book are designed to be easy to implement around writing your book. Let me share some of the secrets to make blogging easy for you.

Develop and repurpose your content

I suggest that you develop and repurpose your content and knowledge in your blogs. You don't need to reinvent the wheel. Jot down the things that people tell you they want to hear from you and answer their questions.

It makes it easier when your message is aligned as you'll probably blog about things related to your book, which makes great material. You can get feedback from your readers, develop intrigue in your upcoming book, and give more detail on particular topics. If time is tight, you don't have to write from scratch. React to topical newsworthy items and write a blog post detailing your take on the topic.

CASE STUDY
Sheryl Andrews
author of *Manage your Critic – From Overwhelm to Clarity in 7 Steps*

My client, friend and now colleague, Sheryl Andrews, The Strength and Solution Detective, first attended my writing retreat in Spain in 2015. She then published her book in the autumn of 2016. She used her blog, networking, and video to build her followers by starting her writing journey.

Although it might feel like a distraction, Sheryl says "It helped me to develop some of the concepts in my book and it meant I was much more effective when it came to blogging and communicating online. I really had to think about who I was writing the blog to. This resulted in some great feedback and helped me to develop my own style of writing."

By producing impromptu videos, where she talked from the heart, she was able to use her own words. This helped her to bring the book together as well as marketing and building interest in her book. This led to her successfully pre-selling her book prior to its official launch.

CASE STUDY
Jenny Phillips
author of *Eat to OUTSMART Cancer*

Another example is Jenny Phillips, who I mentioned earlier. She took a slightly different approach to her book through blogging.

When she started to write her book, she did so by writing multiple blog posts. She found that it was easier to chunk down her content into smaller pieces of writing, rather than focusing on writing the whole book at once.

She then used these blog posts in the relevant sections in her book. This helped to save her time, as she could multi-purpose the great information she'd written for her subscribers and use it in her book.

If you're a natural writer, you'll probably find blogging easy, and you may have already blogged for years.

I've had a blog since I started out in business in 2006 and my blog has most recently helped me to write this book. Where I've written relevant articles, I've been able to bring the content into the book and develop it as necessary to fill in the gaps.

If you don't blog already or you're sporadic in your approach, you might wonder why it's important.

There are many reasons why I love blogging. It's a great way to find your voice and start to share your message. When you talk about things that are relevant to your book, it helps people to engage with you, especially when you invite them to comment on your writing, share your wisdom, and potentially become your client.

It's relatively easy to add a blog to your website, especially if you have a WordPress site, and if you enjoy writing – which I hope you do! – this is a perfect way to share your message with more people.

If you're not already convinced, blogging can help you to get more followers in your area of expertise. When you align your blog to what you're sharing in your book, that's when the magic happens. You won't need to seek out new content because you already have relevant things to write about. You could simply take a section of your book and expand on it for your blog, or blog about something that later gets added to your book.

By repurposing your blogs into your regular newsletters, on your social media platforms, and potentially also in your book, you can reduce your marketing effort. This is a process that I use. I write a weekly blog post and then often use this for my weekly newsletter. I also write social media updates based on each post, but more about that later.

Create your blog ideas

If you are struggling to find ideas for your blog, then let me give you some guidance.

- One thing that inspires my writing – in both my blogs and my books – is conversations I have with clients and prospects, as I'll often answer their questions and concerns via my blog. Then this also means that I have something relevant to send to them and continue to build this relationship.

- If you've carried out a survey or questionnaire or even interviewed people, then you can use this information to inform your blogs. You could answer the most common questions or difficulties that they are facing.

- Think about the biggest problems that your clients and prospective readers are struggling with, and then write about them.

You could also follow Ginny Carter's advice in this short article.

 FIVE POWERFUL BLOG POSTS TO PROMOTE YOUR BOOK LIKE A DREAM BY GINNY CARTER

If you're like many people you've probably struggled to come up with ideas for your blog from time to time. You might even have sat down at your keyboard one day and thought, 'That's it – I've run out. What do I do now?'

Don't worry, we all get stuck.

It helps when you realise there are different types of blog post for promoting your book. Once you've got your head around them, exciting ideas will flow as you see how you can tackle your topic in new ways. Here's a basic run-down of five of them:

1. The how to

This does what it says on the tin. You tell your readers how to do something they find hard and you find easy, on a subject related to your book. This is the most common kind of post.

2. The interview

This is where you interview various experts on a topic related to your book. The great thing about this is it gives you an excellent excuse to contact influencers in your niche; if they like what they read they'll also share it on social media, and by doing so spread the news about your book.

3. The case study

This post tells a story which 'proves' the points you make in your book. Giving an example of someone else who succeeded by following your methods lends your expertise extra credibility. You can link the case study to your book in a couple of ways: by re-purposing a story you already tell in your book, or by writing a new story related to it.

4. The list post

What resources would your readers need to get the most out of your book? How about creating a long list post which gives them links to everything they need? You can refer back to your book within the post so your blog readers know where to go to find out more on the subject.

5. The why post

As the name suggests, this post examines the causes of one of the issues you've written about in your book. It's more reflective, and sometimes more challenging, than the 'how to'. In this you delve into the problems troubling your readers, offering your wisdom on the causes, and suggesting solutions.

In fact, once you hit on a great topic which relates to your book and resonates with your readers, you can write about it again and again using the different formulas above. This is a brilliant way to become known for your expertise and for your book to shine.

Ginny Carter, The Author Maker, is a business book ghostwriter, book writing coach, and author. Find out more at www.marketingtwentyone.co.uk.

One of the things that I do is to record every idea as it pops into my head – sometimes on the back of an envelope, a sticky note or anything else I have to hand! Sometimes this is when I'm speaking with a client or friend; at other times it may be something I've read that inspires me. Evernote is also a great tool when all you have to hand is your smartphone and don't have a pen and paper – I find I'm often inspired at the gym, so I can record my ideas rather than lose them! This means that I have a constant source of ideas to refer to when I'm writing a new blog post.

I'll also write blogs when I'm inspired, and often write multiple blog posts in a day. To help me to become inspired, I transfer my ideas into a Word document, which allows me to create the relevant blog when I'm ready or when I have a specific relevant promotion that may link to a blog post. As I usually write a new blog post every week, this is an important part of my own ongoing business marketing strategy. I was recently advised to have an annual plan for all of my blog posts, which admittedly I don't do, but I've always got a plan that is linked to my upcoming events and themes that I want to talk about.

Break down your topic

For blogging, break down your topic ideas into small chunks. For example, I could easily write an article about marketing a book, but where would I start and where would I finish? I could easily write an article about using blogging to market a book, but again this is a big topic. So I could break this down into sub-articles. Here are some examples:

- How to find the right keywords for your blog

- 5 ways to get your blog noticed

- How to use your blog to attract more clients

I'm sure that I could break down many of these into smaller chunks too.

How to write your blog posts

Whilst this is not a book specifically about blogging, I'd like to share a few tips on writing your blog posts.

Write about one topic, and get your reader's attention with a great headline, one that communicates your message to your reader. Be specific and tell people what they are going to get from reading your blog post. Like with your lead magnet, your blog title may be towards in the way it is framed, for example, 'How to get noticed with your blog' or away from, such as, '5 reasons why your blog post won't get read'.

Whatever your headline, make sure it attracts attention. A 'how to' title may work if you're giving an answer to one of your reader's burning questions. Another headline option is to ask a question that is intriguing to your readers (or even controversial!), or use numbers in your blog title as in 'The 5 most important steps to xxx'.

The copy in your blog post is also important. Like with your title, you also want to continue to engage your readers throughout your article. I'll often write my blog posts and move paragraphs around once I've done the first draft to do this.

Many people may scan your post, so having regular headlines and sub-headlines, important text in bold or underlined, and lists or bullet points, can help you to get across your information clearly. An image or two adds visual interest to the post.

From a word count point of view, I'd suggest you write in the region of 500–700 words for each blog post, but write as many words as you need to get your message across. Oh and don't forget to proofread it!

End with a call to action. What do you want people to do next? Do you want them to leave a comment, give you a call, sign up for a webinar, or buy a product? You will probably have different calls to action for different posts, depending on what action you'd like people to take next.

It's important to think about your SEO. Use keywords strategically if you want your blog post to be found on the web. The Google Keyword Planner tool is one way of finding out what people are likely to search for on the internet.

You may also choose to use a free SEO tool like All in One SEO and Yoast, both of which are WordPress plugins that help you to measure your SEO effectively. I particularly like Yoast's traffic light system that allows you to see at a glance whether your blog post is optimised. It looks at your keywords, page content, image titles and meta descriptions to help you to get more organic traffic to your website.

One of the purposes of your blog is to build your community, as well as sharing great information. Make sure your sign-up box to your lead magnet is on the right of each blog post or 'pops up', so that it's easy for people to sign up and join your mailing list if they are interested in what you have to say.

Lastly, make sure you blast your blog out to everyone who needs to read it, and ask people to share it for you. There are various tools that will do this for you automatically, such as Buffer, and you can add a social sharing plugin to the bottom of each blog post. Proactively send it out to your mailing list and your social media contacts as part of your ongoing communication. I suggest you share your blogs multiple times, not just once you've written them. But if doing this as well feels like another onerous step, then follow my next secret!

Create an editorial calendar

One of the things I do is create an editorial calendar. This easy to create system means that it's easy to regularly share my blog posts. This means that I'm not constantly reinventing the wheel when promoting my messages. Although this may sound grand, all I do is keep a spreadsheet with all of my blogs recorded on it. The spreadsheet has four columns.

The first column details the date that the blog is published. In the second column I insert the title, and in the fourth column I will record the web address of the specific blog post. I copy this row five times.

Then I fill in column number three. In this column, I create at least five different updates that I can share on social media, allowing me to repurpose this blog post in many different ways.

Let me give you a real-life example. I've written a blog post called 'What makes a good book title'. These are three of the updates that I've written to promote this blog post:

- How to make an impact by choosing the right title for your new book

- Writing a book? Make sure you choose the right title. Read my blog for some tips

- Why your book title is essential to the success of your book

This means that when I schedule my social media posts on a regular basis, I'm not searching for new things to share. Each blog post is shared multiple times over months if not years, as there's always a slightly different slant to the overall message. You can download your own editorial calendar at www.librotas.com/free so that you can easily get started.

Become a guest blogger

If starting your own blog at this stage is a step too far or you want to reach a new market, another option is to be a guest blogger for complementary businesses that share your target readership, or create LinkedIn or 'ezine articles' that you share on external sites. If you go down that route, make sure you can include a strong biography, professional photograph and link to your website or book.

CASE STUDY
Louise Wiles and Evelyn Simpson
authors of *Thriving Abroad*

Two of my clients, Louise Wiles and Evelyn Simpson from Thriving Abroad, have written a blog for a while, but through their new book they are looking to reach a slightly different market.

One strategy that they have taken is posting articles aimed towards the corporate market on LinkedIn. They have carefully decided on potentially contentious subjects and have written about these for their ideal clients. Then they follow up with those who like and comment on the posts, thus reaching more of the people that they'd like to speak to.

They have also recorded podcasts which are aimed towards their individual clients, and found that interviewing other experts has been a great way to engage readers and build the Thriving Abroad community. Both the articles and the podcasts will

make great content for a membership site which
Louise is launching alongside the book.

THINGS TO THINK ABOUT

If blogging isn't part of your marketing strategy, then I'd advise you to think about including it.

Don't reinvent the wheel by continually creating new content; just find ways to repurpose what you know already. Share snippets from your book to get feedback from your readers.

Choose to take a helicopter overview on a subject or go deeper into a smaller topic.

Keep a record of all of your ideas, even if you don't write about these topics now.

_____

_____

_____

_____

_____

_____

_____

_____

_____

CHAPTER 6
Publicise with podcasts

As you're a writer, you may well prefer to blog, but if that's not really your thing, then let me offer you an alternative way of getting your message out there. Consider marketing your book through podcasts.

Podcasts are audio products containing short snippets of information that you can share with your audience to listen to on a regular basis. They can last anything from 2 minutes to 2 hours, but are generally around the 10–20 minute mark. They're a great way to provide content, and share your expertise and knowledge with clients and prospects, without needing to be in front of a camera.

You might wonder why you should choose this option, especially if blogging is more your thing. As I mentioned in chapter 1, the purpose of this book is to give you options, and if you're the type of person who would prefer to verbally share your message, then you'll want to read on.

The main advantage of podcasts is that you can reach your existing audience and a new audience through iTunes. Although podcasts are not a regular part of my book marketing strategy, I do enjoy doing them on an ad hoc basis.

My first book, *The Secrets of Successful Coaches*, was born out of 11 interviews with successful coaches. When I launched the book, I also carried out over 20 interviews with other experts that helped to support the book's launch. I often carry out interviews with my clients when they've launched their books to chat about their challenges and successes, and also to help their book to reach more people. Podcasts are a great way to share your own information and also collaborate with other experts and share your knowledge with both communities. You can listen to some of my podcasts at www.soundcloud.com/librotas.

Before you say 'Yes, I'm going to start recording podcasts', find out whether your clients will actually listen to them. If they are busy people and like to listen to great information on the go, then it's certainly something to consider.

The first thing you might be thinking is 'What do I talk about?' Think about what topics your audience would like to listen to – you can follow some of the strategies in the blogging chapter for this.

Think about the top 20 questions that people ask you, as this will give you really good content for podcasts, videos and blogs. You also might want to think about the top 20 questions that your prospects and clients should be asking you but don't!

The thing about podcasts – and video for that matter – is that it allows you to share your knowledge in a different way. People can hear your voice (or see your face with video), and get to know you in a way that blogging doesn't do so well, creating the 'know, like and trust factor' faster.

If you decide to create podcasts as part of your book and business marketing strategy, like blogging, I suggest you do them regularly, as people will come to expect them. When you have a process and structure in place, it will make it easier to implement. When you have standard intro music, a standard introduction, the main body, and standard outro music, this will save you time and give you a consistent approach.

You'll need a decent microphone, a hosting site (PodBean, SoundCloud and Blubrry are three good examples), and ideally you want to choose a hosting site that allows you to connect to iTunes.

You need a way to record and edit the recording, such as Audacity, which will help you to produce the end product. Alternatively you could choose to outsource the recordings to someone who can do it easily, or use a professional studio to record and edit your podcasts, giving you time to write! Although this will impact on your budget.

When your podcast is on iTunes, it will help you to reach a wider audience, as this is where most people go to subscribe to podcasts. They will search using keywords just like they would on an internet search engine. It is also good practice to tell your community about each new podcast that you record. You can do this through social media, your blog, newsletter, or even share a visual image on Instagram or Pinterest.

You may choose to name your podcast series in line with your book or the theme of your business, so consider this before you start. Have an album cover (a small thumbnail of your podcast programme) that will catch people's eye. You could choose someone on Fiverr or PeoplePerHour to create this with relative ease and without spending much.

The advantage of podcasts is that people can listen to them when they're walking, running, driving, on the train, or even doing the washing up! You want to give good content but not massive depth, something that is on an informational level and ideally in bite-sized chunks. You may choose to script your podcast or put together an outline; it really depends on your style and which you prefer to do.

One final note about recording podcasts, as with any form of recording: Your voice needs to be animated. Unlike video, people won't be able to see your expressions so take this into account. If you know that you want to do podcasts, start by subscribing to other podcasts. See what you like and can relate to, and what you think your prospective listeners will enjoy. Podcasts will help you to reach a worldwide audience, so take this into account with your message.

If you don't want to record podcasts yourself, be willing to give interviews for other people instead. Over the years, I've done many telesummits, online conferences, and interviews. These have given great content for my community, helped me to reach more people in other people's communities, and built my credibility.

Here are some additional tips from Alison Colley who is using podcasts to promote her business and her upcoming book.

HOW PODCASTING HAS HELPED MY BUSINESS BY ALISON COLLEY

Podcasting in the UK is still a fairly new and unknown thing, and as a result it is less crowded than other forms of marketing. Depending upon your business or niche you may even find that you are one of only a couple of people in the same area of expertise.

I have been podcasting as a method of promoting my business for two years and I have made many new connections and extended my reach to a wider and different audience. It has increased my credibility as an expert in my field and has given me something different or unique to talk about with clients, contacts and potential clients.

Here's my advice if you want to build podcasting into your business:

1. Be consistent

Like many other forms of marketing you have to maintain consistency and show up on a regular basis. In the early stages, when your downloads are low and you are not receiving any feedback from listeners, it can be disheartening, but as long as you are enjoying doing it keep going, for a minimum of six months to a year, in order to get a real idea if it is going to work for your business.

2. Use podcasting to improve your confidence

Aside from the benefits to the business I have also found that podcasting has helped me to develop my public speaking skills, as whilst you can easily edit your podcast if you make a mistake, you will find that mistakes become fewer as you grow in confidence and perfect your style. This in turn gives you the confidence and experience when standing up and speaking in public.

3. You can do it on a budget

The good thing about podcasting is it is inexpensive and easy to get started. You only need a computer, microphone and internet connection. Whilst good quality sound for your podcast is crucial, you don't need to spend lots of money and can purchase a suitable microphone for £20.

So if you have something to say and are thinking about it, listen to some other podcasts to see what works and what doesn't, and then just give it a go!

Alison Colley is an employment law solicitor specialising in all aspects of employment law and HR. Alison's podcast is The Employment Law & HR Podcast which can be found on iTunes, Stitcher and online at www.adviceforemployers.co.uk/podcast.

You can also listen to an interview on the topic of podcasts on my download page www.librotas.com/free.

THINGS TO THINK ABOUT

If you enjoy talking, then podcasts may be a good addition to your marketing, but remember you don't have to do everything I suggest.

Think about the top 20 questions your clients are asking you, and the 20 questions that they should be asking you. Then answer these in your podcasts.

Your podcast can be published on iTunes, allowing people to find you easily, which will help to build your community.

You also may wish to interview other people or be interviewed, both of which will allow you to collaborate with other experts and serve both of your communities.

_____

_____

_____

_____

_____

_____

_____

_____

CHAPTER 7
Go viral with video

When you're creating content, recording videos is another option. If you enjoy being in front of the camera, then this will be the perfect opportunity for you. If, like me, you struggle to get your message out in one take, then you may choose another way to share your wisdom!

Now, don't get me wrong, I love video. I know it's a great way to connect with people, but there's a time and a place as far as I'm concerned. Some people find it easy to plug in their smartphone, record a piece to camera, and then upload it to YouTube in minutes, or the really brave are happy to use platforms like Facebook Live or YouTube Live. I'm not one of these people! Yet put me in a green screen studio with some well-formed scripts, and I can record quite a few videos in a short period of time.

As with podcasts, videos are a great way to create a connection with your audience – when it's done well. There is a visual element to your message, but you don't need to be the person in front of the camera to create great videos. Other ways to use video online are through SlideShare (PowerPoint with voice-over), VideoScribe (animated cartoon with voice-over) or recorded videos via Camtasia or webinar.

But if you like to be the star of the show, when you have a good script, good lighting, a good video recorder, and you're looking good, then this is a great option to take!

How to use video

You may choose to use video in any of the following ways:

- An introduction to you on your website (which I highly recommend as people can get to know you very quickly).

- An introduction to your book that you put on your sales page.

- On your lead magnet or events page where you can tell people about it.

- As vlogs (video blogs), sharing snippets of information just like a written blog or podcast.

- Marketing for events and workshops, with snippets of you delivering your content and great testimonials.

- Record longer pieces of material that you may share with your audience as part of a freebie or paid-for video series.

- Record an event that you can sell later and to people who have attended.

I'm sure that you can think of other ways you can use video too!

My book launch for *The Mouse That Roars* was videoed, as were two of my events. My talk for the book launch is on the speaker page on my website, so those interested in having me speak for their groups can see me in action. The event videos with testimonials make great marketing tools to share online and show how other people have benefited from attending the events.

I also recorded a video series in the spring of 2016 where I shared my top ten tips for writing a book. These have made great blog posts and are now a lead magnet on my website.

I'm sure you'd love your videos to go viral. To do this they have to be interesting, intriguing, and potentially controversial. The best person to tell you how to create compelling video is my own video expert, Mark Edmunds, who is also writing a book on this topic. You can also listen to an interview I carried out with Mark at www.librotas.com/free.

SIX STEPS TO CREATING COMPELLING VIDEOS BY MARK EDMUNDS

The most important stage of creating any piece of marketing is the planning, and it's exactly the same with video – regardless of whether you're talking to camera or creating an animation using VideoScribe.

Often when a business owner creates a video for the first time they spend too long playing with the shiny stuff: the camera and the editing software. Conversely they spend little time on the two most critical elements of the video: the script and what they actually want to achieve.

Before starting on your next video, follow these six steps, and you will create a compelling video that actually has the chance of being watched all the way to the end.

1. Why you are creating the video

The most important thing you need to know is why you are investing time, money and energy in creating videos.

What is its purpose and how is it going to help you and your business?

What do you want your audience to do when they watch the video?

What does a successful video project look like?

Knowing the answer to these questions will help you formulate the right message.

2. Who are you targeting?

A common mistake in all marketing is being too general. Being general does not work as you cannot specifically appeal to everyone.

So you need to know your target audience. Who are they, what do they look like, what are their problems, what do they do, where do they shop, what are their goals in life, what are their trigger points and what do they want? The more you can narrow it down to your perfect or ideal client avatar, the better!

The clearer you are at understanding who you want to work with, the easier it will be for you to formulate a script to talk about their problems and desires using their words, terminology and language patterns. This means they are more likely to be engaged by your videos because they feel you understand them and what they want in life.

A great way to get results is to create a 'client avatar' of who you want to work with and then give this a real name and persona, such as 'Sarah', a single mum in her thirties, who lives locally and has a specific interest in your area of expertise. Then it allows you to create a mental picture of them in your mind.

3. It is all about them

Now you know what you and your ideal clients desire, it's time to start formulating your message either in the form of a 'word for word' script to use on a teleprompter, or a series of carefully planned bullet points to keep you on track when ad-libbing to camera. However, before you get carried away thinking about what you can tell your viewers, remember one thing: Your viewers will not care about you and your message when watching the video. Instead, when they first watch your video, all they will be thinking about is themselves and how they are going to benefit.

When crafting your message, ensure that they will gain something, whether that's an understanding of how you could help them, or even something actionable that they can use to achieve something in their business or personal life straight away.

4. Use spoken language and do not try to be perfect

If you are writing a script to use on a teleprompter remember that you are creating something to be spoken aloud. Therefore throw the grammar book out the window and write 'spoken English'. Use abbreviations, put pauses in as though you are thinking (um, err), start sentences with 'and', keep your language simple, and make sure your script is easy to read out loud.

This last point is critical as it will prevent you from wasting time and money tripping over your own tongue and feeling highly frustrated because your videos do not sound natural. Being conversational, umming, erring and occasionally making the odd mistake in your videos is a good thing as it will make you more believable and authentic to the viewer more approachable as a person.

5. Speak to one person

Your videos will be watched by many people – hundreds, thousands, tens of thousands – and, with luck, many more.

However even though many people will watch them, you will get a better level of engagement if you create your videos as though they are just for 'one' important viewer. This is because everyone who fits with your 'client avatar' will have a sense that it's a personal message for them and that they are special rather than just part of a larger online audience.

Speak to this one person (remember 'Sarah' who I mentioned earlier?). By doing this, you will find it an easier experience for you than trying to engage with a cold piece of plastic and glass also known as a video camera. In addition, your videos will be far warmer and easier to watch for your audience.

6. Write your script

There are many different ways to script your videos. One of the simplest is the Hook, Path and Persuasion technique, which consists of three parts:

Part 1. The hook: grab their attention

You only have a few seconds to gain the attention of your target audience, so make sure your script starts with a bang! Grab them by demonstrating you understand the exact problem they want to be rid of or give them a fact which makes them sit up and think 'I need to know more!'

Part 2. The path: take them on a journey

Now you have got their interest, you need to keep them engaged by taking them on a logical journey towards the most important element of your script – the call to action. On this journey give them enough information so that when they get to the end of the video they feel they can trust you and want to follow your call to action. To do this, your video needs to address their 'perceived' problem and show that you can help them solve it.

This may be through education on what they need to do (but not how to do it); by demonstrating how you have helped others through success stories of other clients; or by actually solving their problem in the video but then introducing a bigger and far more scary problem.

Part 3. The persuasion: tell them what to do

Finally you need to get them to take action by telling them to specifically do something. Failing to do this means that they are likely to watch the video but then move onto something else ... such as the next video of a cute kitten or a kid falling off a skateboard on YouTube or Facebook.

Tell them to 'pick up the phone and give me a call to discover xyz' or 'share this video with your friends because y' or 'sign up for the event today and you will get abc extra'.

Remember to use scarcity to get the best results by giving them a reason to do it NOW. Otherwise they are likely to procrastinate until they forget about you.

Mark Edmunds, Shooting Business, helping businesses build brand reputation and gain more clients through video testimonials and business event videos. Find out more at www.shootingbusiness.com.

Hosting your video

With video, you also need to think about where you host it.

YouTube is free but it has its disadvantages. I'm sure that you've wasted many hours sitting down to watch one video, then getting distracted by the next one that YouTube then decides to show you!

However, the advantages with YouTube are that well-watched videos show highly on internet search rankings. There are things you need to think about to do this. You need good quality videos with a strong headline and keywords, which are shared regularly.

Having a high number of subscribers will also help your videos to get noticed. Be aware that search engines can't rank what you're saying, so include your script in the information box when you upload your video, and then your video is more likely to feature.

There are other options for video that you do need to pay for, although they are certainly better for videos that are part of a paid-for programme. These are Amazon S3 and Vimeo Pro (the latter of which costs around $200 for a year), but are great for hosting webinar video recordings, promotional videos and video blogs, as they can be set as private and don't have adverts or lead on to the next unrelated video.

Lastly, you can also share your video directly onto Facebook, which will help you to reach more people, especially if combined with a Facebook advertising campaign. I'll share more about this in chapter 9.

Are you going to do video as part of your book marketing?

If so, what next steps are you going to take?

Please do subscribe to my YouTube channel and watch some of the valuable videos on there – www.youtube.com/karenwilliamssdc.

THINGS TO THINK ABOUT

A great script, good lighting and a decent video recorder will be a good starting point to creating an effective video.

There are many ways you can do video, from Facebook Live, to picking up your smartphone, to recording a professional video in a green screen studio.

As with any form of marketing, a consistent approach is important.

You need to grab people's attention from the moment they watch you, and remember to include a call to action that tells people what to do next.

_____

_____

_____

_____

_____

_____

_____

_____

CHAPTER 8
Become a webinar whizz

One of the things that I've done regularly in my business is hold webinars and teleclasses, the latter of which I used when I started out. I've run over 100 since 2006 and they've been good strategies for both my business and my books.

In a nutshell, webinars are 'a seminar conducted over the internet' and I'll share my top tips in this chapter. But before I move on, let me tell you the difference between webinars and teleseminars. Webinars tend to be web based where people generally dial in via an internet link (although many do allow your subscribers to use the telephone if they prefer) and you can run a slide show – and share your webcam if you wish – at the same time as running it.

Teleseminars or teleclasses were more popular before webinars came into existence, and are generally telephone based only. You also may have heard of the term telesummit, which I mentioned briefly earlier. These are virtual events which are similar to a business conference where many experts are invited to come together and educate attendees on their area of expertise. The big difference is that a telesummit is a virtual event rather than a physical conference. Telesummits are great to use in conjunction with your book if you want to get in front of new audiences and interview others who will promote the event with their audiences.

The commonality between all of these different things is that they are online, virtual events, and people can listen in from all around the world. The benefit of this, of course, is that you can create a worldwide audience of people who will get to hear about your expertise and your book. And you don't need to go out or dress up to run them!

There are a range of webinars products that are available to use. GoToWebinar™ and Zoom seem to be the most popular in the UK; the former starts from £89 plus VAT per month at the time of writing. Some webinar platforms have a 30 day free or low cost trial period so that you can try them out, and others allow you to run free webinars, although you'll get limited functionality.

For teleseminars and telesummits, one of the most popular platforms is Instant Teleseminar. In addition, there are other options available that allow you to do something similar, for example some programmes work in conjunction with Google Hangouts via Google Plus. Some will cost you and not cost your guests, and others are free, but there will be a call charge for those attending.

You might be thinking: 'I can blog, I can do podcasts, I can do video; why do you recommend webinars?'

The reason I like webinars is that you can provide great value for your clients for a low cost, and it's another way to showcase you and your valuable content. It's a great lead magnet to grow your list when you offer a free webinar, and when part of a paid-for programme, it's an effective way to deliver content.

As a webinar is usually live, you can interact in real time with your attendees all around the world at the same time. You can share great content and answer their questions. You can also record it and have a product that you can give away or sell later, and it could also become a podcast!

That's why it's a great way to build your business, grow your list and develop your credibility alongside writing your book.

If you're wondering how you can use webinars specifically, here are a few suggestions:

- Informational masterclasses where you teach content and showcase your expertise, which links in well when you're building your community and telling them about your upcoming book.

- Preview webinars where you give valuable content, then upsell to a product, programme or event – or book!

- Interviews with complementary experts where you can showcase their expertise, adding value to both of your communities, or being interviewed by someone else where you do the same. It will help you to reach more people, and these could become podcasts or videos once recorded.

- Paid-for programmes, memberships or mastermind programmes where you can use a webinar platform to provide content-rich value. You may do this in the pre or post-launch stage, and I've given some examples of how I've done this in the third section of this book.

If you've never run webinars before, try them out with some trusted friends before you go live! There's nothing worse than facing problems when you're inexperienced. There are things that could go wrong, but if it helps, I've faced most of them!

- I've been live when my internet has crashed and has gone on 'go-slow'.

- I've had to cancel a webinar when my internet didn't want to work.

- I've managed to mute myself so no one could hear me.

- I interviewed someone live, and their internet went down, so I had to fill in the time before they eventually came back onto the call.

- I've forgotten to press record and now I write a note to remind myself every time I run a webinar!

- I've also pressed 'record' only to find out later that it hasn't recorded properly and there has been a system error.

The only way around the technicalities is to practise and just do it. Don't be fazed when things go wrong. If the worst comes to the worst, it's a great excuse to run your webinar again!

If there are other things that might concern you apart from the technicalities of doing it, I'll address some of these in this chapter.

Streamline and structure your topic

It is important to choose the topic of your webinar wisely, like you would do with any event, blog or programme. Start with the end in mind. What do you want people to do after watching your webinar? For example, if you aim to upsell to an event, what do people need to know first? Then make sure your message is relevant. For example, don't run a webinar on '3 ways to manage stress at work' if you are promoting a programme on 'How to write a CV'.

When you start with the end in mind, it will help you to streamline your content, and work out what you're going to cover. I suggest you stick to three or four points that you are going to be covering in the webinar, and make sure that you're answering a need that your ideal clients and readers want to hear from you.

Think about how much content you can fit into your proposed time slot. As I've run so many webinars, I can pretty much gauge exactly how much content I need to cover in an hour and how many slides I need to deliver this. I'm normally spot-on give or take a couple of minutes! If you're wondering how long your webinar should be, remember that people do have a limited attention span, so don't make it so long that people stop listening.

If you are using visuals, keep your slides to headlines, a few bullet points and pictures. Include stories, case studies and testimonials if they add value to your content and provide great social proof. Remember to include a call to action. With some webinar platforms you can also use your webcam, but I personally believe this can also slow down the performance of your presentation.

On a practical note, I think it's important to know your material but not be too prescriptive. I use PowerPoint notes and print them out, but that's because I like to keep myself on track. I find it very easy to go off topic, especially if I've been asked a question, but the notes do tend to bring me back to the content.

One difference between running a webinar and a physical event is that you cannot gauge the reactions of your audience, which may well faze some people. That's why it's really important to build connection early on with those on the call. There are two things I like to do. Firstly, I like to ask regular questions for feedback. Attendees can reply by 'raising their hands' which you can see on the dashboard, or by making a comment in the question box. Secondly, I like to ask for questions that are relevant to my talk. Then it's your choice whether you reply to them during the webinar or at the end. These are both great ways to interact with your audience.

If you're worried that you won't be able to answer the questions on the hoof, then you could ask for questions in advance of your webinar. If you're not sure that people will ask you questions, have a few up your sleeve, so that you don't feel silly if no one asks any during your webinar.

One important thing to note if you are making an offer, for example, you are upselling from a free programme to a paid-for product or event, do tell people about this in the introduction so that people are expecting it. And include a bonus for immediate action.

How to promote your webinar

The reason I haven't talked about this first is that you need to have an outline for your content before you write your sales page. I'm going to be talking about sales pages in more detail in chapter 11, but specifically for a webinar, you need to:

- Have a compelling headline or ask a question that creates intrigue, controversy or interest (remember AIDA?).

- Choose a subtitle that your audience will identify with, which may focus on their problem or what they want instead.

- Give people a reason to sign up – even a free webinar needs to sell! Oh and don't forget the sign-up box.

- Make sure you have persuasive copy written with your ideal client in mind, which will probably talk about their problems and how your webinar will solve them.

- Add social sharing buttons to make it easy for others to share the details of your webinar with their friends.

- Have a short biography to enable you to start to build a relationship with those who don't know you, and this should demonstrate why you are the best person to help them.

- Include some client testimonials to show your audience how you work.

- Include a countdown to your webinar start time if your software allows you to do so.

If you're wondering how to persuade people to sign up for your webinar, you do have to have good sales copy, but you also have to promote it widely.

If you've already got a mailing list, then promoting it to your community is a great place to start. But don't just think you can send one email and people will sign up. Some people will miss your emails, and I generally send a sequence of three emails with different copy to encourage people to sign up.

There is a fine line between giving people too much notice and too little notice to attend a webinar. I will normally start promoting a webinar 5–7 days before it's due to run. You might also wish to give people an incentive to be live, as few people will listen to the recording. This could be a checklist or PDF which supports the material that you are sharing.

Do try and find other people who are willing to be involved with its promotion. Joint ventures or affiliates will help you to reach more people, and some people may be willing for you to do a webinar solely for their list. Although be prepared to pay a commission if you're promoting a product or event off the back of your webinar.

Use a combination of methods: social media, blog, podcasts, and videos to help promote your webinar. Talk about it in many guises to persuade people to listen in. Facebook events and advertising are also tools that I generally use.

Deliver and wow your audience

At this stage, I'll assume that you've created your content, developed your slides, and you've had people sign up for your webinar.

I'll also assume that you've planned your promotion if applicable and have some stories and testimonials to share with your audience.

Here are a few practical tips to make sure your webinar runs well:

- Warm your voice up first and have a glass of water to hand.

- Create a quiet environment, so that you're not going to be disturbed.

- Ideally use a headset, as this will hopefully avoid background noise.

- Remove distractions, and ideally have someone else on hand to answer any questions.

- You may choose to have a backup recorder in case of any problems.

- Make sure you're comfortable before you start!

Then you need to deliver, delight and wow your audience!

How to use webinars to promote your book

You can use webinars at all stages of your book's promotion. At the pre-launch stage of your book, you will be credibility building. You'll probably be using free webinars to build your list and develop the awareness of you and your expertise.

If you choose to run a programme alongside your book or after you launch it, then webinars are a great way to deliver paid-for content.

You could also have what's called an evergreen webinar which is recorded once but delivered many times. It looks like a live webinar to those who sign up, but actually it's pre-recorded and can be promoted via a Facebook advertisement to grow your mailing list or perhaps sell a product. It's certainly a good timesaving tool, although personally I prefer to deliver webinars live.

You could also have a webinar as a virtual launch for your book, instead of holding a physical party.

Lastly, when I was writing *Your Book is the Hook*, I wrote it alongside running an online paid-for programme. This was delivered via a series of webinars. Although I mention this in more depth in chapter 20, it's also important to note it here. That's because this approach was part of my pre-launch strategy. It enabled me to promote and sell an online programme before creating the content, and this allowed me to write the book quickly and easily. It was also one of the strategies that I used that helped to generate over £16,000 in income from the book before it was actually published. If you'd like my support with webinars, or indeed any of the strategies in this book, please email karen@librotas.com to arrange time for a chat.

 **THINGS TO THINK ABOUT**

Webinars are a great online tool at any stage of your book's promotion, whether you want to build your community, sell your book, or promote a product or programme.

Test out the platforms before you get started or seek recommendations from your colleagues and friends.

When developing your content, start with the end in mind. What do you want people to do after they've watched your webinar?

Always remember to multi-purpose your content. You don't have to reinvent the wheel when you're creating the material for your webinar!

_____

_____

_____

_____

_____

_____

_____

_____

CHAPTER 9
Go strategic with social media

When you want to create a solid author platform, social media is usually a core element. Although online marketing shouldn't replace offline marketing when promoting your book, it makes sense to use it to its full advantage.

I believe that social media is a good way to complement the other suggestions already offered to you in this book, rather than being used as a standalone tool. Although which social media platform to choose is another thing altogether!

As I mentioned in chapter 1, if you are seeking to go down the traditional publishing route, one of the things that a publisher will look for is great connections: a big list and many thousands of social media contacts. But even if you're going down the partnership or self-publishing route, which I explained at length in chapter 13 of *Your Book is the Hook*, I suggest you do this anyway. Not only will this raise the profile of your book, it will also raise the profile of your business.

At the time of writing, the main platforms for social media, in my opinion, are Twitter, Facebook and LinkedIn. Many people also use Google Plus, Instagram, Pinterest and more. In this chapter, I'll be giving you a brief overview of each of the three main platforms.

You probably know which platform your ideal reader prefers to use. This will help you to decide where to spend your energy and time, and which one should give you the best results.

On a personal note, I have a presence on all three of these main platforms, and they all work for me in their own unique way, but my preferred one is Facebook. I find it easy to connect with those in my community, engage with my ideal readers, share my advice in groups where my readers hang out, and I've found that Facebook advertising is a great way to promote my business.

Each social media platform requires you to have a good profile, which sells what you do and tells people about your book!

Twitter

Twitter is a micro blogging platform and is a great place to connect with like-minded individuals and share your advice. Using Twitter will help you to develop a reputation in your marketplace by connecting with complementary businesses or prospective clients.

With Twitter, like your posts, your profile needs to be succinct. What I like about Twitter is that you can connect easily with people. Developing an interest in others, and sharing their posts, will help you to build a relationship online.

Twitter is also a great way to connect with prominent people. When I wanted an influential entrepreneur to write the foreword for my second book, *How To Stand Out in your Business*, I approached Rachel Elnaugh (formerly of Dragons' Den and Red Letter Days) to do this, as I knew that she was prolific on Twitter. I sent her a short tweet and this resulted in a great testimonial for my book!

Here are my Twitter tips:

- You need a strong and short profile that positions you as an expert.

- Twitter is great for following and connecting with influential people in your industry.

- You can create short and snappy updates where you can share your tips and demonstrate your expertise.

- You can retweet other people you admire or whose content you value, which helps you to build relationships.

- You can set up lists to keep up to date in this fast-moving environment, and keep an eye on those who are influential or interesting.

- You can use and set up hashtags to connect with others on particular topics.

- You can watch the hashtag #journorequests to keep an eye on stories that journalists are seeking, and respond to those relevant to your business or tag others when it's relevant to them.

I also asked Twitter expert, Nicky Kriel, to share her top tips.

 TOP THREE TIPS FOR USING TWITTER BY NICKY KRIEL

The biggest mistake that I see authors making is that they wait until their book is ready to be published before they think about marketing their book on Twitter. Their feed becomes a frenzy of 'buy my book' tweets. It never works!

So assuming you don't want to be one of those authors, here's what I suggest you do in preparation for your launch:

Start early

Start developing your Twitter presence now. Make sure you start tweeting regularly every day. You want to share content that is helpful and useful for your ideal customer. Always put yourself in the shoes of the people reading your tweets.

Make sure you include that you are writing a book in your Twitter profile. Ideally, your book is connected to what you do in your business. Tip: #AmWriting is a hashtag that authors use.

Build a community around you

You want to build a relationship with potential readers and influencers before you get close to the book launch. Actively find people on Twitter who you think will be interested in your book in the future, follow them and start chatting to them on a regular basis. A good way to be systematic about having conversations is to put certain people into Twitter lists. This will help you to focus on people that you consider to be important.

It is also very useful building relationships with other authors so that you can talk about book writing. You would be amazed how helpful people on Twitter can be. A few more good hashtags for you to find fellow writers are #AmEditing, #WordCount, #WriterWednesday, #WritersLife. A creative hashtag to try that will help you get your book written is #1K1H (one thousand words in one hour). You use it before you sit down to write and it helps keep you accountable, especially if you can get another Twitter writer to do the challenge at the same time.

Use storytelling

All good stories start with the hero (that's you, by the way) accepting a challenge to go on a journey. Along the journey, the hero has an adventure with a number of challenges, and in a decisive crisis wins a victory (your book being published), and then comes home transformed in some way. The most interesting part of the story is always the journey. You are going to have challenges as a writer getting your book out of your head and into the real world. When you share these conflicts, detours and blocks, you take potential readers with you on your path. The lovely thing about Twitter is that you only have to share your journey in small bites (140 characters).

Remember: If you can share pictures along the way, it's even better. Images on Twitter get more visibility, engagement and retweets than text only tweets.

Say hello to me @NickyKriel and if you are new to Twitter, you are welcome to do my free Twitter mini course to get you started. www.nickykriel.com/free-twitter-mini-course.

Nicky Kriel is a social media coach and trainer and author of *Converting Conversations to Customers* and *How to Twitter for Business Success.* Find out more at www.nickykriel.com.

Facebook

Facebook is seen as the social network where people are more likely to share their dinner and personal pursuits, yet many people fail to realise how useful Facebook can be to business and their book.

Most people have a personal profile, and this is a great starting point if you want to use Facebook. You can connect with your friends and business contacts, and share relevant information on your page. It is important to note that as a business building tool, Facebook frown on sharing lots of business content on your personal page. And if you're worried about your business connections getting to know your personal business, then you can set lists to manage your privacy settings.

That's why I advise that you also have a business (or fan) page. You could, if you wish, also have a business page solely for your book or for you as an author!

Having a business page allows you to share information about your business and your book, and build a community of people who love what you do. You can share book reviews, give away snippets, and share your tips to those who like your page. The only downsides are that the Facebook algorithms now mean that only a few of your fans will see your messages, although you can advertise your posts to reach more people on your business page.

Do encourage people to join your mailing list and don't just rely on social media to help you to build your community. You have no control over the changes they may make in the future and the impact this could have on your business.

I use the Facebook groups function, and have private Facebook groups for clients and members of my programmes. It's a great space to ask questions, voice concerns and celebrate successes. You could offer something similar for your own programmes or for people who have bought your book.

You can, of course, also contribute in other groups. Bearing in mind the rules of the group, they can be great places to ask questions, answer questions, connect with others and, if permitted, tell people about your new book.

I asked two of my business colleagues to share their thoughts on Facebook. The first is Suzii Fido who shares her tips for Facebook advertising and the second is Louise Craigen who talks about using Facebook without adverts. Personally, I believe that using the strategies in conjunction with each other will help you to maximise your Facebook reach.

SIX REASONS WHY FACEBOOK ADS ARE THE SMART OPTION BY SUZII FIDO

Are you on the fence about Facebook advertising?

Are you worried that it will be too expensive and not get the results you want?

We all know that an active presence on social media is key for the success of any business and with 1.71 billion active monthly users (July 2016), Facebook is the mother of them all.

It's becoming increasingly difficult to be heard and with an average of only 2–5% of your page followers even seeing your posts, it can feel like an impossible task. That's where Facebook advertising steps in.

Facebook advertising gives you the loudspeaker to shout across the noise and help you stand out and it doesn't have to cost the earth to do it. We have successfully achieved a great return on investment for our clients for a small daily budget (under £10 in some cases). Still on the fence? Let me tell you the main benefits of Facebook advertising.

1. Cheap

When you compare it to other marketing strategies, Facebook has always come out as the cheapest advertising platform available. You can create ads for as little as £1.00 per day and still get results!

2. Greater reach

For a small budget you can reach literally thousands of prospective customers and with 47% of Facebook users accessing via mobile, you can even reach them on the go, unlike TV advertising which is very costly.

3. Laser targeting

With hundreds of Facebook demographics available including age, gender, marital status, location, job position and interests to name just a few, you can really laser target your advertising to your ideal client at a fraction of the cost compared to other media formats. For example, if you are a solicitor in Portsmouth offering assistance for asbestos related injury claims, you can choose to only target individuals within a particular radius of Portsmouth between the ages of 25–65 with a job position in the highest risk areas. With this much detail, you are far more likely to gain enquiries from the customers you seek and get a great return.

4. Remarketing

Adding a Facebook pixel to your website gives you the ability to remarket your website visitors within Facebook. This can give a great return on investment as they clearly have an interest in your product/service if they have looked you up so when you create adverts to this specific audience they are already 'warm'.

5. Testing capabilities

When you are advertising it's always advisable to test different options e.g. images, wording, audience etc and with Facebook advertising this is very simple. With the statistics showing which ads have attracted the desired outcome you can quickly see which is performing better and change the lower performing ads to constantly improve your results.

6. Measure results

There is no point in running a campaign if you are not going to measure the results and adapt your campaign accordingly. With the statistics page in Ads Manager, it's very easy to see so many different statistics from cost per click, how many people reached, age and gender of the responses, device used and much, much more, giving you valuable data to help you make accurate decisions on both the current and future advertising campaigns.

Suzii Fido, Marketing with Ethics, helping to increase the brand awareness of ethically focused businesses and organisations using the power of internet marketing. Find out more at www.marketingwithethics.com.

SMART WAYS TO USE FACEBOOK
BY LOUISE CRAIGEN

Did you know that there is a lot you can do to grow your Facebook organically? It will take hard work and persistence, but I promise you, it will be well worth it. The most important thing to remember is to talk to your followers and you will then get likes, shares and comments in return. Here are my top tips to help you.

1. Being consistent with your posts is important, even if you are not yet getting engagement. Make sure you post regularly and do schedule to save time. You can post manually as well when something newsworthy or interesting happens.

2.   Videos have become an extremely effective way to get people talking on Facebook and there are many apps to help you create useful, helpful, amusing and entertaining videos. Alternatively, share videos that appeal to you.

3.   Be adventurous and do try new stuff; it sometimes takes trial and error to see what kind of things will work for you.

4.   Once you are blogging regularly make sure you use LinkShare to post a link to your most recent blog at least once a week – use a picture or the blog headline to grab attention, ask a question or share advice.

5.   Posting quotes is often a useful way to give an insight into you, your personality, core values and beliefs. Use quotes that are relevant, inspirational, motivational, entertaining and amusing.

6.   Remember to put a call to action on some of your posts, where relevant. It might be a phone number, asking people to share, or just requesting a response. Also, ask for likes, shares, input and feedback in your posts as often as possible.

7.   Surveys and competitions will boost your Facebook reach. You can have a lot of creative fun with them, and they can also be used as a lead generation tool if you ask the right questions.

8.   One of the best ways you can help your Facebook is to cross-promote it with your other social media platforms and other marketing tools. Post a link to your Facebook page on your Twitter page and vice versa. Do this regularly on Instagram, Pinterest and LinkedIn as well.

9.   Spread the Facebook word in print as well; put a 'like us on Facebook' on your emails, flyers, posters, letterheads, compliment slips, leaflets, adverts and practically anything you print for your business.

10. Keep your posts varied and relevant to your industry and your customers. Make sure you answer any questions and be flexible. Use statements from your business to share your passion and knowledge and give helpful hints and tips.

11. Something I have had success with is Facebook groups. First you need to search local groups where your potential customers are. Then you join, use your personal profile and offer help and advice. You need to get known in these groups as helpful and engaging, and do read the terms and conditions on each group admin page to see what kind of business promotions are allowed. Post links to your blog, website or newsletter and promote your business. Several groups have days when they invite members to post a link to their business Facebook page, so you will get great exposure that way as well. Keep it light, fun and as entertaining as possible.

Here are a few reminders for you.

- Make sure you link back to your website/blog/newsletter as often as possible and schedule your posts to save yourself valuable time.

- Remember to use Facebook insights; these will help you know when to post and show you the best performing posts.

- Check your notifications at least once a day and keep the conversation going. Before you know it you will be expanding your Facebook reach and gaining valuable, interesting new and engaged followers, without paying for ads.

Louise Craigen from Platform Social helps small business owners to run their social media effectively and efficiently. Find out more at www.platformsocial.co.uk.

To conclude this Facebook section, here are my own tips:

- Facebook is a great place to connect with people you've met at events and continue to build this relationship.

- It's an informal network, which often works for small businesses as long as you're careful with the information you share.

- You can showcase your expertise and knowledge through your business page and groups.

- You can set up events and invite people who you know may be interested.

- You can share your knowledge in groups, answer questions and build relationships with members.

- Facebook advertising allows you to target people very effectively to grow your list and promote your programmes.

- Take the approach of sharing and not spamming, otherwise you'll upset people who are connected with you, are the admin of other groups, or even breach Facebook's terms and conditions. I'm sure that you don't want Facebook to shut down your account!

LinkedIn

LinkedIn is generally used to develop professional relationships online. There is a different etiquette to other social media networks, and there is an underlying tone of connecting for mutual benefit. It is great for meeting new people or building relationships with those you have already met.

There are many ways in which you can use LinkedIn to promote your book. You can connect with people in the organisations where you'd like to do business further, and at a glance you can see which of your friends has connections with those you may wish to meet.

Like Facebook, LinkedIn has a group facility where you can connect with people, ask and answer questions. You can also post articles in LinkedIn, where you can share relevant information with your audience.

Having a strong profile header, comprehensive job history and endorsements will support you in this area.

I asked LinkedIn expert Naomi Johnson to give you some tips.

ESTABLISH YOURSELF AS AN AUTHOR WITH YOUR LINKEDIN PROFILE BY NAOMI JOHNSON

LinkedIn provides another great opportunity to get your book out into the world and establish yourself as an expert, and your LinkedIn profile is a vital piece of your toolkit. With Google ranking LinkedIn second for any name-based search, you simply can't afford to leave it incomplete or poorly finished.

Added to this, your LinkedIn profile is where you have the opportunity to connect with your entire business community, past and present work colleagues and perhaps friends and family. These are all people that you'll want to inform about your book and your new status as a published author.

There are many parts of your LinkedIn profile where you can feature your book so think carefully about how best to do it. If you've written the book to generate leads, you'll want to make sure the profile outlines your full product eco-system and paints a full picture of what you do and how a prospect can work with you.

Here is a quick overview to get you started:

- Add a PDF excerpt of the book to your profile with a 'Buy Now' button embedded in the text linking to your shopping cart or Amazon.

- Create a slide presentation showing the cover, the key text and reviews, and again add the 'Buy Now' button.

- Create a promotional banner for the top of your profile.

- Add a new entry in Experience with the title 'Author | [Title]'.

- Mention it in your summary.

- Use one of the three website links in Contact Info to lead to your sales page.

- Use the Publications section to feature your book.

- Reposition items on your profile so the book is heavily featured.

- If writing with others, use the Projects section and tag each other.

To get further tips, examples and support implementing the above, go to the free resources section on Naomi's website.

Naomi Johnson, expert LinkedIn profile strategist and author of *What to Put on Your LinkedIn Profile* and *Grassroots to Green Shoots*. Founder of www.theprofile.company.

LinkedIn tips

Here are some more tips and ways to use LinkedIn to promote your business and your book.

- Update your profile to make sure that it reflects your key skills and add 'Author' to your profile.

- Make sure your professional headline tells people what you do and how you help them, rather than your job title.

- Update your status regularly and do share your progress with your book.

- Share relevant articles on LinkedIn that fit around the content of your book and ideal readers.

- Seek endorsements for your book through your connections.

- Ask your clients to give you a recommendation and also recommend others who you've worked with.

What to post on social media

When you've decided your best approach on social media, it's time to decide how to use them most effectively. Here are some of the things that you can do:

1. Tell people about your book

The obvious thing to do is to tell people about your book. Give your subscribers regular updates, give them a chance to read a snippet, and share your highs and lows.

2. Ask for contributions to your book

If you are looking for other experts to contribute to your book, like I've done in this one, using your social media contacts is a great way to do this.

3. Share your blogs, videos and podcasts

I'm sure you realise by now that your message in your business and book needs to be consistent, so sharing your content via blogs, videos and podcasts is essential.

4. Turn your wisdom into pictures

Tools such as Canva (www.canva.com) or Photoshop have made it much easier to turn your written word into visual pictures that you can share online. Many tools like this have free or low cost versions that you can use, although this may give you limited functionality.

Simply take your own quotes and tips from your blog or your book and use these tools to create them. Add your name and web address onto them, which will be shared when they go viral.

5. Turn other people's quotes into pictures

If you don't yet have your own quotes or tips to share, (although I'd question this!), you can use other people's quotes that are in the public domain. Remember to attribute the quote to the right person, and add your web address or logo.

6. Share your tips

You don't have to put your quotes into pictures. You could simply type them into Twitter, Facebook, etc and share them with your followers. These would be short and sweet snippets and you could finish by adding the website address for your book.

7. Share reviews and tell people how they can buy your book

Once you've published your book, share reviews of your book, as other people's opinions will sell your book without you needing to promote it.

8. Tell your followers about other updates

You could also share other things that you're doing. For example, LinkedIn is a great place to tell people what you're up to each day, and you can share information like your next speaking engagement, media coverage, videos of you speaking about your book, podcast interviews or other relevant information.

How to make social media simple

If you're starting out in social media, or don't have much time, there are some tools that can help you. I currently use a scheduling tool called Hootsuite, although there are other options available.

They generally have free and low cost versions, and which one you choose will depend on the functionality you require.

If, like me, you use multiple social media platforms, but prefer one over the others, then you might be loath to miss the others out. Scheduling tools allow you to plan posts on one or all of your social media accounts. Although please do bear in mind that the different social media platforms each favour a different type of approach.

If you created an editorial calendar as I mentioned in chapter 5, this will be easier for you. Weekly or monthly, you can schedule your posts for the coming period, and that means that you'll always have interesting content to share with your followers, without having to be online in real time. Although Facebook does prefer it if you schedule posts directly onto your business page, this keeps your presence in people's minds.

Social media etiquette suggests you can post on your Facebook business page once or twice a day. You may post on Twitter multiple times, and share what you're doing professionally on LinkedIn.

Even though this information is in the pre-launch part of this book, this is something that you need to be doing regularly. Consistent content will help you to build your contacts, likes and followers, and as you develop your book, you'll develop more specific content that you can target towards your ideal readership.

Social media platforms give you a great way to reach more people with your book, but they do take time to build – and they can be a time suck! Although scheduling regularly can be effective, there's something that's equally important about real-time interaction.

 **THINGS TO THINK ABOUT**

Choose to use the social media platforms where your clients hang out and post regularly.

Social media is a great way of reaching new people and connecting with those who you've already met.

Although you can schedule posts and updates, real-time interaction from time to time will better engage your audience.

Use your time wisely, otherwise you'll never finish writing your book!

_____

_____

_____

_____

_____

_____

_____

_____

_____

CHAPTER 10
Cultivate your connections

When promoting your business and your book, it's easier when other people are interested in your work and are willing to shout out about it. So far in this book, I've talked about online marketing, but it's important to meet people face to face too.

Many authors are introverts, which may be why they have decided to write a book, but you can't spend all your time behind your computer! Getting out into the real world is very effective, and if you're smart, you can combine the two. I enjoy going to networking events, but equally I'll use social media to connect with those I meet. This enables me to keep in touch with them and we can support each other.

This chapter is all about cultivating your connections, and developing your community offline, mainly through networking. I've included it in the pre-launch section of this book, as it does help to build relationships before you publish your book, but the tips equally apply at the launch and post-launch phases too.

Create networking opportunities

To develop your connections in the real world, networking with others is a great starting point, as you get to talk with people. The lack of real conversation is one of the downsides of social media in my opinion. When you can talk with people, you can tell them about your book ideas and get their feedback. Most importantly it's a great opportunity to find out about them, and build a relationship which is mutually beneficial.

When I talk about networking, this includes formal networking opportunities and events where you may share your 60 second elevator pitch and mingle with other people like you, where I do hope you'll mention your book! That's why having a short introduction that grabs people's attention is important, as well as having a longer elevator pitch that can be varied depending on the situation. But remember, when you're having conversations, we do have two ears and one mouth for a reason! When you give your elevator pitch remember it's all about the listener not you – tell a story, give examples of how you work, and have some sort of call to action so that the listener knows how they can approach you for more information.

Most people who are successful in business do networking on some level, whether they choose to go to larger events or workshops, or attend local networking groups. If you're not doing some sort of networking, then you're definitely missing out. As well as spending time with others – a must if you're working on your own – it gives you the chance to meet new people. If you find networking a struggle, perhaps you've not yet found the right one for you, as different groups work for different people. Once you've found one that works, however, attend on a regular basis so that people can get to know you.

The purpose of networking isn't to sell. Not in my eyes anyway. The purpose is to build relationships, have conversations, and this may later lead to a new client or a referral. Remember if you're in a room of 40 people, you're not just talking to those 40 people; you're also talking to their contacts who may need your help.

Due to my own networks, it's not unusual for someone I know to connect me with other people I can help and vice versa. On a personal level, many of the people I now work with as colleagues were once people I met through networking events. I've referred people who now work with each other, and I've recommended people to connect, and being able to help others is important to business – and book – success.

The thing a lot of people miss, when networking, is the follow-up. It's all well and good having some great conversations and filling your desk drawer with business cards (we all do it!), but it's important to connect with mutually beneficial contacts. I don't mean adding someone to your mailing list without permission; I mean dropping your new contacts a short email, connecting with them on LinkedIn or requesting to add them as a Facebook friend.

As well as physical networking, I advocate less formal things too, as these also help you to build your networks. I'd include things like meeting people for coffee, Skype conversations with people who you've connected with face to face or online, telephone conversations, and asking for connections within the area you want to influence with your book.

There is huge value in doing things like picking up the phone and talking with people, as with our reliance on technology, this is something that is seldom done today. What can you do that your competitors may not?

Let me put it this way. The more people who know about your book, the better. People know people, and if someone isn't in your target readership, they may know someone who just has to get a copy once your book is published. Then get their details!

EXTEND YOUR NETWORK

Who do you know who might know someone who would be interested in your book?

_____

_____

How can you get in touch with them?

_____

This isn't necessarily your ideal readers either. You might want someone famous or influential to endorse your book, so how can you connect with this person? I went to an event in 2010 run by product creation expert Peter Thomson, and during the lunch break I approached him to write the foreword for my first book. And he said yes!

The reason I've included networking in the pre-launch phase is because writing your book will put you in a different league from your competitors – even before you've finished it. That's why getting clear on your message and telling people that you're writing your book is a good thing to do before you've published. This will raise your credibility and authority and may influence those you meet.

If you're in the early stages of writing your book, you may also be doing some market research, and this is another area in which your contacts may be able to help you. If you want to interview people for your book or contribute articles, then having great contacts will enable you to tap into their content – just like I've done in this book!

Here are a couple of examples of how my clients have used their books to develop their networks, reach more clients and raise their credibility before they've been published.

CASE STUDY
Louise Wiles and Evelyn Simpson
authors of *Thriving Abroad*

Earlier I mentioned Louise and Evelyn, authors of the forthcoming book *Thriving Abroad*. The book is aimed towards supporting corporate employees who have been asked to move abroad by their employers.

During their pre-launch phase, they interviewed executives in corporations where they would love to work with their staff. This was a strategic choice. They knew that the interviews would make good content for their book and give the organisation's opinion on the topic. They also knew that saying that they were writing a book would put them in a different league to competitors. It gave them the chance to get in front of the decision makers who might choose to use their services having seen how they work.

This is one of the reasons why when everything you do is aligned to this one ideal client and readership, it will make it much easier to grow your business. Then when the book is published, there will be a reason to reconnect with these interviewees.

CASE STUDY
Jeremy Glyn
author of *The Inside Track*

I've also been working with Jeremy Glyn and his new book *The Inside Track*. He has been writing a book to appeal to a new market where he has considerable expertise, and his plan is to use this book to reach more people in this area.

During the latter stages of writing the book, he started to reach out to those who he wanted to support with his book. He found that this led to making some tweaks to his book copy as he understood what people wanted to learn from him. It also led to him creating manuals and training programmes for the different steps of his process, developing lead magnets that would help him to promote the book on his website, and making changes to his website to appeal to this ideal audience.

Although this slowed down the completion of his book, it helped Jeremy to be clearer on what people wanted to know and how he could best serve this client group.

With both of these examples, if you don't ask you don't get! But do be specific in what you're asking for!

The other advantage of face-to-face and online networking is building relationships with people as well as a great community. Just a word of caution: Remember that networking and creating relationships is a two-way thing; what can you do to help others too?

Develop joint ventures partnerships

It would be great to have as many people as possible sharing your launch and helping you to reach more people and, of course, helping you to get more sales. You might decide to do what I often do, and that's to invite complementary and sometimes competing businesses (I know, it's a bit of a shock, isn't it!) to contribute to my books with their expertise. My view is that we are all there to support each other, and there is enough room for all of us!

Creating formal or informal joint venture partnerships is something that is important for most businesses if you want to create more success at any stage during your book's writing, publication or marketing.

Speaking opportunities

I've included my tips on speaking in chapter 21 in the post-launch phase, but equally you may find that this is a good strategy before you launch your book. Like networking, it is a good way to connect with people who need to hear your message, and a great way to showcase your expertise. If you do seek speaking opportunities at this stage, it is a good way to find out what your readers want to hear before you've published it, and there's nothing stopping you from pre-selling your book before it's even finished!

THINGS TO THINK ABOUT

Make sure that networking is part of your book marketing strategy, whether you attend formal events or have informal meetings.

Remember that networking is a two-way thing. What can you do to help others in your network?

Building your community is not just about getting readers for your books and new clients; it's also about developing relationships and getting feedback.

Start to write a list of people who can help you with the launch of your book.

_____

_____

_____

_____

_____

_____

_____

_____

CHAPTER 11
Pre-sell before publishing

Selling your book before you've published it may feel like a scary thought, but it does have multiple benefits, especially if you're on a budget and would like to bring in some money to pay for your publishing. There are two ways of doing this: pre-selling your book personally, and crowdfunding. In this chapter, I'll give you advice on the former to help you to get pre-orders for your book to make this easy and not overwhelming!

Encouraging people to order your book before it's published is something that is good to do if you a) want to create a buzz for the book early on, b) want to generate some income for publishing and marketing, or c) both. It also might give you the impetus you need to finish it! This is how you can do it.

Buy your book's website domain

The first thing you need to do, once you know the title of your book, is to buy the website domain for your book's title. There are a couple of reasons for this. Firstly, it's easier to say "You can pre-order my book at www.bookmarketingmadesimple.com" rather than www.librotas.com/thetitleofyourbook. I'm sure you can see where I'm coming from! Secondly, it enables you to direct people to your page so that they can get more information about your upcoming masterpiece.

If you have a web address for your book, you can still link this from your main website (and if you don't know how to do this, ask your web designer!). Not only is having a book web address more memorable, it also gives you the chance to see if anyone else has written a book of a similar name or if someone else is using this branding. By the way, if you can't buy the exact web address, you may choose the name of your book with the word 'book' or .book on the end. If you're like many of my clients, you've probably already got a bunch of website addresses that you've accumulated during your time in business, so adding one more is easy!

If your budget is tight, at the very least have a page on your website solely for your book. This will allow you to start promoting your book at this early stage.

Create compelling website copy

Once you've got your website address, it's time to create compelling copy to tell people about your book.

If you've already read *Your Book is the Hook*, you'll have learnt in chapter 12 about creating a powerful synopsis for your book, and I touched on this earlier too. This is essential if you're looking at traditional publishing, but equally important if you are going down the partnership or self-publishing route. This will help you to develop a strong pitch for your book.

One of the advantages of writing a synopsis is that this will help you to create your compelling copy. It'll be easy for you to delve into the problems that your ideal reader is facing, who you are, and how you can help them through your book. Also, if you've done the exercise in chapter 2, then you'll be clear on this anyway. Just think of this webpage as an elevator pitch for your book.

If you're creating a standalone website for your book, I suggest you use a tool like the Squeeze Page Toolkit or Leadpages to help you to create it. You may find this easier than creating a WordPress site or other structure behind the page unless you have a specific theme that makes it easy to do this. Ideally you need a one page site to avoid having a menu or anything else that might distract someone from pre-ordering or buying your book.

When you create your one page website, here's my advice:

- Start with a strong headline that's going to capture your reader's attention. Although you may want to mention its title and subtitle, this isn't the thing to start with!

- Then tell people about the book, tapping into some of the difficulties that your ideal reader is facing.

- Next tell your reader about the book, why you wrote it and how it will help them.

- If you prefer, you could record a video with this information, and include some bullet points outlining the main points on the page underneath the video.

- If you already have your cover design, you can also add a 3D or 2D mock-up cover of your book on the page. You can replace it later, once your book is published, with a photo of you with the book.

- Once people have started to read your book, do include their endorsements on this page. This is great social proof from your readers of what they've enjoyed about your book. One thing that I do is get feedback from a few people in my community in the latter stages of writing my books, and you can ask these people to endorse your book, and you can also do the same for high profile endorsements.

- If you don't already have reviews for your book, you may wish to include relevant client testimonials instead.

- Share a little bit about you with your professional photograph. Then people can get to know who you are as well.

Although you need a way of taking payment on the page, I don't believe that it needs to be complicated and expensive. When I pre-sold my third book, *Your Book is the Hook*, in 2014 as an experiment to see if this worked, I simply added a PayPal link behind a buy now button on the page.

If you do decide to pre-sell your book, you may find that doing crowdfunding or holding an Amazon bestseller launch as well is difficult, unless there is a long time lag. Your list and community probably won't appreciate you promoting your book to them more than once. However, if you have a good joint venture team in place for the latter, then you might consider doing this, as you'll be relying on your team to help you to rise up the Amazon charts.

In my experience, it's important to start promoting your book at the right time. I suggest you wait until you are clear on your launch date to do it. A good time is when your book is being edited and proofread. You'll have a little more time to focus on this part of the process, and you'll be pretty clear about when your book will be ready.

When you're pre-selling your book, be realistic with your distribution date and make sure you tell everyone who has ordered it, as there may well be a time lag between taking orders and having it ready for distribution. If there is a slight delay (like I had with *Your Book is the Hook* in 2014), then update your buyers. I gave away a few chapters via PDF to people who had already bought the book to whet their appetite in advance of its publication.

In the early days, you're likely to be distributing the book yourself, unless you outsource it to someone. Once the books arrive, you'll have a production line going on in your office where you'll be packaging up the books. What I love about doing this myself is that in the past I've been able to add the wow factor with personalised mini chocolates and I've also signed the books, something that was still mentioned by my clients over a year later.

When you have a system in place to distribute your book, it will be easier. I have some brightly coloured jiffy envelopes, a standard letter in place, postage readily available, and labels ready to print the address when an order comes in.

When promoting your book, the best people to share it with are those who you've primed for it – as long as you've done many of the other things I've suggested!

If you want people to order your book in advance of its publication, give people an incentive. This might be a special discounted offer and you may also include bonuses which have some scarcity. You may include an exclusive webinar, report, download, video or audio recording ONLY for people who pre-order within a certain date period.

It is a great way to keep people appraised of where you're at with the book, and to create frenzy before it's published! From a business point of view, if you're feeling brave, you could also upsell to a higher priced offer after someone has bought your book, which I'll explore later on.

Now something to add to this point. You can still use this page after you've launched your book. Although you'll probably use Amazon to distribute your book, you may choose to offer a signed copy through your website, or have a special offer for those who have signed up to your lead magnet. All you'll need to do is tweak your content.

For an outline of some of the resources that I use and useful websites, please go to www.librotas.com/free for more information.

CASE STUDY
Sheryl Andrews
author of *Manage your Critic – From Overwhelm to Clarity in 7 Steps*

I introduced you to Sheryl earlier. Before she had a website to promote her book, Sheryl took an innovative way of promoting it. At her mastermind group she happened to mention that if she really thought people were waiting for the book it would motivate her to finish it. At this point two of the members literally threw her cash and said they wanted to read it. This prompted her to post on Facebook which resulted in 25 other people also wanting her book. She had so many people asking for her book that she had to keep a record on her whiteboard to remind her who had said they were interested. And every one of them bought a copy.

This was a great incentive for her to finish it, and a great incentive to create a page where people could easily buy it!

THINGS TO THINK ABOUT

Pre-selling your book is a great way to create frenzy and a buzz whilst you are finishing it.

Be realistic with your timescales as the final parts of publishing may take a little time as you have less control if other people are doing this stage for you.

Add an incentive for ordering your book early and post it out with a little something that gives it the wow factor.

Keep it simple; tell people about the book and add social proof in the form of reviews from people who have already read it.

_____

_____

_____

_____

_____

_____

_____

_____

_____

CHAPTER 12
Crowdfund your book

When I was in the final stages of this book, I considered crowdfunding it. The main reason being that I didn't feel that I could mention something in this book if I'd not done it myself. Then I did my research and found four lovely ladies who were willing to share their advice, and I must admit, after receiving it, that I decided not to follow this route!

However, if you are struggling to fund your book, want to raise its profile with a bigger audience, and already have a community of people who want it, it may be a good way to go.

Traditionally crowdfunding has been used by individuals and companies who are seeking funds for a big project. It is also becoming increasingly popular for authors who want to fund their book. If you've never come across the term before, crowdfunding is 'raising finance for a project by asking a large number of people each for a small amount of money'. There are many platforms available, including Kickstarter, Crowdfunder, and Unbound, which is specifically for authors, where they will also publish your book for a fee.

There are many pros and cons, which my contributors will share in this chapter. The main advantage in my view is that you can reach more people through a crowdfunding platform, but you do need a large community already. However the major disadvantage is that if you don't raise the funds for your book, then you won't be able to launch your project, although you will have raised your profile by getting your message out there.

Ellen Watts is one of my clients, working with me on her second book, *Get it Sorted*. For her first book, *Cosmic Ordering Made Easier*, she went down the crowdfunding route. Although she wasn't successful in meeting her crowdfunding goal, it did attract more clients. She learnt a lot from the process and plans to crowdfund her next book. Here are her top 14 tips.

 TOP 14 CROWDFUNDING TIPS BY ELLEN WATTS

1. Choose the platform that suits your needs – There are choices of crowdfunding platforms; some guarantee the money but those generally have a higher % fee; others only pay out if you reach your target, otherwise the deal's off. Personally I chose the latter because I liked having the target and the 'all or nothing to play for' feel. I thought it was fair and also had the potential for excitement. After some research, I chose Kickstarter for my project and would choose them again.

2. Follow the instructions and the advice on the site – Complete the profile page in full, and include pictures and the story of why you wrote the book and who it will help. Use the expertise of your crowdfunding platform as they'll have run hundreds if not thousands of campaigns. They know what works and what doesn't.

3. Choose your time frame carefully – Shorter campaigns get more momentum, but give yourself enough time for the word to get around. I was impatient on my first one and chose three weeks, but I wasn't really ready to get promoting. A few distractions meant the campaign failed, and it didn't raise the funds I'd set as a target. Now I plan to set my target for around 12 weeks.

4. Make a video – It doesn't have to be fancy; just you talking is fine, but if you have a mock-up of the book or other props, so much the better. People need to connect with you as the author and hear your passion for your book.

5. Don't set your target too high – With crowdfunding, it's better to set a slightly lower goal than you'd really like and bust it sky high, than set a stretching one and miss it. So I suggest working out your real goal i.e. how much do you really need to be able to create your book and get it published, and then set your crowdfunder for the minimum you need to make that happen. Then set up another goal just for you which is twice as much and aim for that. Then, if you hit 50% of your secret goal, you will have had a successful campaign in your crowdfunders' eyes and will get paid the money, but chances are because your focus was higher, you will sail past the 50% with ease!

6. Don't expect the donations to come from friends – You don't want to feel you're nagging your list or family and friends to death, although if your offer's good enough, you shouldn't need to. The sweetest surprise for me was how much traffic came from the Kickstarter community itself. There are people on there looking to help, plus get bargains and exclusive inclusions. Doing a crowdfunder is a great way of building your list if you're ready to take advantage.

7. Have a range of offers including ones that don't cost you much in time or effort – I included tiny ones like for £2 they could get 'a special report' which was not available anywhere else. I also had a £5 one 'My Top 20 Cosmic Ordering Tips' sent as an A4 PDF – PLUS a special thanks personal video message explaining the tips in a little more depth.

Having these small starter investments meant anyone could support me and feel they'd contributed even if they didn't have a lot of money. They don't have to be shipped – so all the funds raised are profit – and you only have to do the PDF or video once and it can be repurposed later.

Likewise, have a couple of very high end offers. These are likely to take up a good deal of your time – like a VIP day – so make only a few available and you don't need many to reach your total. Don't hold your breath expecting this to be taken up, but remember if it's not listed they can't pledge for it, and having it there gives your book some credibility. My top end package at £2,400 or more was my 'Get it sorted apprenticeship'.

8. Showcase your book – In the middle of your offers will be your book itself and possibly your book plus book launch tickets. Again be mindful of numbers and how many you can cope with delivering, and put a maximum number rather than causing yourself a logistic and fulfilment crisis if things should take off wildly. PLUS scarcity often encourages people to take action immediately.

9. Be creative – What backers love most is 'can't buy in the shops' specials, so things like adding their name to a roll of honour in the book, if that's possible, will raise extra funds with little extra investment on your part.

10. Add up your offers – When all your offers are listed make sure that the total exceeds your target. This seems obvious, but I've seen some campaigns that haven't done this, and there's no way that they can hit their target even if they have sold everything that they have listed.

11. Campaign your campaign – Share it on social media, pop it in your newsletter and email your list, get networking, speaking and mention it everywhere. Get some buzz up around reaching your target.

12. Update your pledgers regularly – Nurture these lovely new contacts and get them into your world as soon as you can via your list and social media.

13. Keep your promises – Broken promises are the number one cause of unhappy customers, so give priority to fulfilling orders soon after the campaign has finished.

14. Even if your campaign is not successful, it is not a failure. You will have attracted and made contact with people interested in your work and had some pledges that you can now follow up outside of the platform. For me, I see very little risk in attempting a campaign other than a little time and effort, but the potential to gain a great deal is very real.

Ellen Watts, www.ellen-unlimited.com, author of *Cosmic Ordering Made Easier: how to have more of what you want more often* and *Get it Sorted – for once, for all, for GOOD.*

I was introduced to Lisa Ferland by one of my clients. She crowdfunded her second book, *Knocked Up Abroad Again*, through Kickstarter, and raised over US$10,000 for the project. She is now focusing on building a self-paced course for crowdfunding publications to help people to avoid some of the mistakes that she made. You can read an article she wrote on the subject at http://knockedupabroad.eu/blog/secrets-crowdfunding-success.

When I asked Lisa for her advice, she told me:

"If you are an established writer with an engaged audience, you can easily surpass a low level target and achieve success. The main thing with Kickstarter is that you're doing an all-or-nothing campaign and are essentially condensing a year of marketing efforts into a short period of time. Every day you need to publish a podcast, a new blog, a guest blog, a press release, a live video, etc. It's an intense process, which is why Kickstarter recommends campaigns only last for 30 days."

Lisa's book was an anthology, with contributions by other authors, which helped the crowdfunding success. But she admitted to me that it became more work than any of them had anticipated and, looking back, she would have given an extra incentive for the contributors to take part in the crowdfunding campaign.

In the four weeks of her Kickstarter campaign, they sold over 300 books (e-book and paperback), which was a great boost for the book. She said: "A successful crowdfunding effort also provides a sustainable model for self-publishers so they don't have to keep dipping into their personal savings. However, the downside of crowdfunding is that if an author is not successful, it can be a huge crush to the ego." She also advised that it will be more successful if authors help each other to achieve collective success. This type of support can be provided by writing guest blogs, sharing the campaign on Facebook, and routinely checking in with the creator to provide moral support throughout the campaign.

I was introduced to Ebonie Allard who went down the crowdfunding route for her book *Misfit to Maven*. She said: "Crowdfunding for me was never about the money. I had hit the first slump in writing where I couldn't remember why I was even bothering. I felt like no one needed to hear my story and no one would read the book. So I coached myself and realised I needed some more accountability and I also needed to get really clear on my why. Plus money is a great motivator, when you're spending all day writing and no invoices are being written, no reward imminent. I used crowdfunding as my personalised carrot to keep me going."

To get started on her crowdfunding journey, Ebonie created a series of videos and chose a crowdfunding platform. She worked out how much she felt would buy the books she needed to do a good first run, and launch her book. But she didn't anticipate how demanding it would be to raise the funds. Here's her advice:

- Have a plan and a daily promotion schedule mapped out before you begin.

- Have an audience to begin with.

- Secure real people who will pledge in the first 24 hours before you go live. You want to tip past 50% of your target in your first day. That way you'll get on the recommended page of your crowdfunding platform.

- Be prepared to ask for pledges way more often than feels comfortable.

- Don't ask for more than you need, but it's better to get overfunded than underfunded.

- Do come up with interesting 'money can't buy' perks. People are not just pre-ordering your book, they're supporting you! Give them something unique and fun for helping you.

- Thank everyone who donates on social media; most people love recognition and it gives you a reason to keep talking about it.

- After you're done, stay in touch with your contributors and give them regular updates.

My last contributor is Nicky Kriel who successful crowdfunded her second book, *Converting Conversations to Customers* – you may remember she shared her Twitter tips earlier in this section.

Nicky decided to crowdfund her book after submitting her book proposal to a traditional publisher. Although her idea was accepted, she soon realised that she couldn't write the book that she wanted to write. She decided at that stage to go down the self-published route as an independent author, realising that she would have to market it anyway.

Like my other experts, after investigating the various crowdfunding platforms, she chose Kickstarter, recorded a video, and asked for the full amount (£3,500) to fund her book.

Here are Nicky's thoughts about the process:

- In the UK people don't necessarily understand what crowdfunding is, so Nicky created a page on her website to provide more information.

- Like the other authors who have contributed to this chapter, Nicky agrees that you need to allow enough time for your crowdfunding to be successful. Nicky was still in the editing stage when she started her crowdfunding campaign. Nicky found towards the end that it was down to the wire and there were many negotiations behind the scenes to reach her target.

- Create a good plan to raise the money, as well as getting people on board to support you before you start your project. Create a big buzz when you launch your book, because it will be more successful when you get the momentum going from the day you start your campaign. Nicky suggests considering using Thunderclap, a crowdspeaking platform (like an online flash mob) that allows you and your social media contacts to share the same message at the same time on your social networks.

- Although you may feel like you're telling people all the time and bombarding them with information about your crowdfunding project, there will still be people who don't know about it. Keep people updated with your progress on your book, both those who have already contributed and those who you think will support you.

- Get support from others. One of Nicky's friends created illustrations that Nicky used to help promote her campaign. She advises using square images, as these work well across all social media platforms.

There are some great tips in this chapter, so if you do decide to go down the crowdfunding route, do follow their advice.

THINGS TO THINK ABOUT

Crowdfunding works when you already have a good community in place and have support from others to raise the funds.

Be realistic with your target, as with many crowdfunding platforms you won't be successful unless you reach your target. There are a few platforms where you're still successful if you don't reach your target, but you will still need to deliver on your promise.

Don't underestimate the time that it will take to crowdfund your book, but you will reap the rewards if your project is successful.

You're more likely to achieve success if you have a great plan to achieve it, and are prepared to hustle to reach your target!

_____

_____

_____

_____

_____

_____

CHAPTER 13
Two more pre-launch strategies

As you can see there are many ways to pre-launch your book. Here are two final ideas.

Author of...

I suggest that you add 'Author of the upcoming book xxx' to all of your marketing materials.

This includes your website, social media profiles, directories, guest blogs, articles, business cards, flyers, and you could also add it to historical articles that you can update. You can also add it to your autosignature, which you put on the bottom of every email. Once you have the 2D or 3D cover and/or book website, you can add this too. This is a very simple, low cost strategy to market your book.

Make sure that you talk about your book to anyone who is interested. It will raise your profile and help people to understand your message.

Approach influential book endorsers

Although technically this doesn't fall under marketing, it is one of the keys to the success of your book. Having high profile names endorse your book by providing the foreword, reviews, or testimonials that you use on the back or inside cover will help your book's promotion. Having a big name publication or three give you a great review will raise the credibility of your book. For *The Mouse That Roars*, I had a brilliant review from Suzy Greaves, the editor of *Psychologies Magazine*, which was great to raise its profile.

I'll never forget the moment that someone at a networking event said that one of the reviews on my website resulted in her buying one of my books. Don't underestimate the power of other people's opinion and how these can positively impact on your potential readers.

To get started with your reviewers, write a list of the people you'd like to get your book in front of, and once you've finished writing your book, it's time to approach them. Actually you could approach people for endorsements at any stage, even after you've published. These can be an excellent addition to a second edition or great social proof for your website page.

Although in a slightly different context, when I wrote my first book, *The Secrets of Successful Coaches*, I wanted to interview specific people who were influential in my field and many people have asked how I got some of them on board. Well, I simply asked them. Where I knew them personally, I contacted them personally and where I didn't, I asked mutual contacts to put us in touch. Of course, some people said no, but equally, some amazing people said yes! You can add stories, case studies, and interviews at any stage before your book is ready for publication.

 **THINGS TO THINK ABOUT**

There are many different ways you can market your book in the pre-launch phase. When you mention it to people it will build your credibility at all stages of your book's creation and launch.

Getting social proof from reviewers and endorsers is an important thing to consider as other people's opinions will have more weight than you promoting your book.

Create a list of people who you'd love to endorse your book and simply ask them.

Look for every opportunity where you can promote your book!

Take a moment now to review what you've learnt from this section. Which options are you going to choose to market your book in the pre-launch stage?

_____

_____

_____

_____

_____

_____

_____

SECTION 2
How to launch your book in style

One of the reasons I've covered a lot of information in the pre-launch section is to set you up for success. When you start to do some of these marketing activities on a regular basis, and have the systems in place to manage them, then it will be easy to keep them going when you launch your book.

By the launch stage, your book will be completed, edited, proofread, well designed, and published. Ideally you'll have both a physical copy of your book and an e-book. If you'd like more advice on doing this professionally, do get a copy of *Your Book is the Hook* (www.yourbookisthehook.com) which walks you through the process.

When you have the physical copy of your book in your hand, I'm sure you want to be ready to sell your book and launch it successfully.

By this stage, as long as you've followed the tips in the first section, you'll have already created a buzz for your book, and have people who are ready to buy it — or have even pre-ordered a copy.

At the launch stage, you may wish to jump ahead and start to introduce the post-launch strategies at the same time, or at least be starting to think about them. But before you jump too far ahead, there are four main things that you need to think about now:

1. Focus on getting publicity for your book.

2. List your book on Amazon, bookstores and other online distributors.

3.   Then you'll probably hold a book launch party.

4.   Later, you may have an Amazon launch for your book to propel it up the bestsellers list.

These four things are the focus of this section and the next five chapters (with some additional top tips) and will give you the strategies to launch your book in style!

CHAPTER 14
Seek publicity and media exposure

You can seek publicity and media exposure for your book at any time. It doesn't need to be something that is confined to the launch stage of your book or something you should forget about after you've launched it. You may find that during its writing you have an article that is the perfect thing for your local newspaper, a national magazine, or you may get approached for a radio or television interview.

Whilst I was writing *The Mouse That Roars*, I secured an interview with a freelance journalist who wrote for the *Daily Express*. Even though the interview took place 18 months before the book was published, it was still a great coup for my business. Not only did I get a double page spread in the paper, but I had a photoshoot specifically for the piece – including makeup, hair and photographer! You can read a copy of the interview at www.librotas.com/free. I found out about the opportunity through a PR friend telling me about a #journorequest post on Twitter, and when contacted, the journalist was interested in the main story that I share in the book.

If you haven't already done any publicity or you want to specifically promote your new book, do think about how you can promote it during the launch stage. Getting into the press and magazines or onto radio or TV can help you to reach a bigger audience with your book.

CASE STUDY
Lorraine Palmer
author of *Raw Food in a Flash*

Lorraine had some brilliant PR success before she published her book. She was published in three magazines: *Chat Magazine, The Funky Raw Magazine,* and *Wolverhampton Magazine,* where she was featured on the cover.

She was also approached by a newspaper wanting to feature an article on her story, and has done two podcasts and one live interview to date. As Lorraine went through the menopause prematurely, this was the hook that interested the journalists.

She also finds that people notice her more and doors are instantly open because they know that she has something important to say. And although she has already had great publicity, Lorraine also knows that greater success is yet to come once her book is released.

When you start to get publicity for your book and your business, create a media page on your website where you can share the links to your pieces. It's a great reminder of where you've been featured and it will also show prospective interviewees how you've come across in other articles, podcasts or interviews. For an example, go to www.librotas.com/media.

I've also got a scrapbook of all the physical articles that I've had published. This has included articles I've written for magazines, pieces where I've been a featured expert, top tip articles and many more. This is a great reminder of what I've achieved and where I've been featured.

Creating a press release

If you choose to go down the traditional or partnership publishing route, your publisher will probably provide an AI (Advance Information) sheet for your book, although creating your own press release (which is similar) isn't too difficult to do.

Although a press release by itself may not get you publicity, it is a good starting point when coupled with a powerful story and clear message. It's important to note that journalists aren't interested in your book. They're more likely to be interested in your *story*. This may be the story behind why you wrote your book, or if your book is autobiographical in style, they may be interested in some of your experiences that led you to where you are today.

A good press release will touch on this story, tell people about your book, and give your biography and details of how people can purchase your book. But it needs to be interesting, create intrigue, and sell you as well as the book.

To achieve success, it's not just about sending your press release cold to a handful of journalists. The best results will be from those who you know personally and have developed a relationship with, and those who resonate with the type of people you want to connect with.

To get the best results you may choose to engage a professional PR expert. This then allows you to do what you're good at and they can do the same. A good PR expert will be able to see angles that you may not see, and the stories that journalists will love. They'll also have a little black book of the right contacts that will get you into the right publications for your audience, and relationships with people who can help promote you. You may find that some of these journalists freelance for a variety of different publications.

If you're doing your PR yourself, access the publications that your ideal readers actually read, and contact the editors and journalists who write relevant articles. If you haven't already got a media list of useful contacts, then it's time to create it now.

Some magazines have a book review section, and you may also find book bloggers who specialise in your area of expertise who will review your book on their website. My books have been reviewed in online magazines, print publications and on guest blogs. My clients and I have also been featured on the TV and radio. Just look out for opportunities and they may simply fall into your lap.

Here is a perfect example: A former client saw a feature on BBC Breakfast and put a post on Facebook asking if any of her friends could connect her with the journalists. Through her contacts, one of the presenters contacted her personally and one of my PR friends informed her who she needed to contact at the BBC.

Sometimes you just need to be in the right place at the right time and be willing to comment on current affairs. You can be proactive, for example, another client approached her local paper with an article about stress management just before National Stress Awareness Day one year, and they snapped up her piece. If your book does have a specific link to a particular time of year or occasion, do remember to use it!

Radio and television interviews

If you're lucky, a great way to showcase your knowledge is by being interviewed on the television or radio. I've done both, and many years ago I had a regular slot on a local radio station.

But if the thought of doing an interview feels a bit scary for you, my go-to publicist, Helen McCusker, has agreed to share her tips on giving your first live radio interview, which were first published in *Self Publishing Magazine*.

HOW TO GIVE YOUR FIRST RADIO INTERVIEW
BY HELEN MCCUSKER

Self Publishing Magazine columnist and Bookollective founder Helen McCusker is not only a book publicist but trained as a radio journalist and used to produce and present on many radio stations across the south coast of England. Here she shares her tips for on-air success when the time comes for you to give your first live interview.

So you're a new author, your book has been published and a radio producer has shown an interest in your story and has asked you to visit their studio to take part in a live interview. If you're like the majority of the authors I work with, you'll be feeling apprehensive and probably a little overwhelmed by the thought of being heard by thousands of listeners.

My background is in radio presentation and news; yes, that's right, I used to spend my working day in front of a microphone... and I used to love it! Radio is fun, and the best part is that you don't see any of those thousands that are tuned in listening to you and they can't see you either (unless of course there's a sneaky studio webcam!). So the best advice I can give you is to treat the interview as a casual one-to-one chat with a friend. You'll enjoy the experience and learn a lot from it for future media engagements.

Preparing yourself

As soon as the interview has been confirmed, post a review copy of your book to the producer with a press release and author biography to ensure the presenter has time to look over it before interviewing you. Note that I say "look over it" – don't expect the presenter to have read it from cover to cover, because they usually won't have had time to.

It's also worth making it clear at this stage what you do (and what you don't) feel comfortable talking about, just to save any awkward silences on-air.

Tune in to the radio station and programme that you'll be interviewed on before your interview day to get a feel for the presenter's interviewing style and the target audience you'll be speaking to. You could ask the producer for information on the demographic and some potential questions that you might get asked.

Write down and practise key messages in a series of bullet points; this includes the title of your book, any supporting websites and your author name too (it's amazing what you can nervously forget whilst on-air, trust me!). Be able to explain what your book is about in a few sentences; many authors cannot do this, so give it a go before the big day arrives.

The day before your interview, confirm the date, time, place and anticipated length of the interview with the producer in charge, just in case there have been any last minute changes to the schedule. Ensure you have their direct telephone number and that they have yours in case of emergency.

Be sure to let your social networks know that you'll be on-air so that they can tune in and offer you feedback; it's also another good excuse to let everyone know that you've published a book!

Arriving at the studio

On the day of the interview, allow plenty of time for the unexpected (traffic, parking space, bad weather, etc.). Most programmes will require you to arrive around 20 minutes before you are due to go on-air, to give you enough time to meet the producer, run through any concerns and grab a coffee or snack (remember to eat beforehand, otherwise a rumbling stomach could prove embarrassing when your microphone goes live!).

Be ready to meet other interesting people in the green room – the room where guests wait before they enter the studio – so take your business cards and do some all-important networking. When your time slot arrives, remember to switch your mobile phone off before you enter the studio and remove anything else from your person that might be distracting for you or the presenter (for example, noisy jewellery!). A glass of water is always useful to keep at hand just in case you have a tickly throat or cough during the interview, so ask the producer if they can organise one for you.

The interview

The most important thing is to relax and be yourself. Remember, you're the expert on your book and you've already proved that what you have to say is interesting, because you've been booked for a radio interview. Sit up straight, listen, talk slowly and smile! It might sound silly, but listeners can sense your emotion from your voice and if you're not talking enthusiastically about your own book they may stop listening.

Of course, your story may be emotional in other ways and, if the subject matter is sensitive, you will need to adjust your interview style accordingly. Have a bullet point list in front of you so you have a clear idea of the direction the interview will take and the most important items you wish to discuss. Your interview will fly by and you don't want to go home with regrets, saying "I wish I'd talked about that!"

The trick is to covertly refer to your book wherever possible; you don't want the interview to sound like one big advertisement, but you can discreetly refer to it when answering questions – a 'soft sell' as such. Perhaps quote a favourite character... or an important chapter. For example, "In my book, *The Author*, I provide ten tips for writing a book. We don't have time to talk about all of these right now, but let me read you the first two..."

If your book is business related in any way then be careful of using confusing jargon, as you need to get your message across clearly and in a relatively short space of time. If quoting statistics, have a summary of the facts in your notes, so you can easily and accurately quote them. Keep your answers brief and to the point as there is nothing worse than a rambling author who doesn't let the presenter guide the interview. In radio, the term 'sound bite' refers to good, informative, snappy answers which convey a point clearly and succinctly.

Towards the end of the interview, have your contact details in front of you to read out: website, Facebook, Twitter addresses and of course, those all-important book details such as price and local stockists.

Follow-up

Radio programmes can usually be accessed online for a short time after broadcast, so why not have a listen back and analyse your interview strengths and weaknesses? Be warned, it can take some time to get used to the sound of your own voice!

Record a copy of the interview and ask the radio station if you can upload it to your website, which they will usually be fine with, as long as you post a full credit alongside. Most radio programmes these days have Facebook and Twitter pages, so ask the producer if a link to your website or Amazon page can be uploaded for listeners to find out more about you and your book.

Finally, send the producer and presenter an email to say thank you, and volunteer yourself for future interviews. It's always worth asking for their feedback too as we all have areas we can improve on and this will prepare you even more for interview number two. Good luck and most of all, enjoy!

Helen McCusker, Bookollective (formerly Booked PR) is a publicist who helps authors to achieve high profile media coverage and boost their book sales. Find out more at www.bookollective.com.

You can probably see that there are many ways that you can get publicity for your book, and the places you wish to be featured will depend on your ideal audience. As with any of the marketing techniques, be proactive, have a plan and make sure you follow up with those people whom you've contacted.

You may have to react to a media opportunity quickly. The trick with being ready for any such opportunity is to know your content well. It's amazing how quickly you may forget the content of your book after you've written it! Have a range of different ways you can share your expertise, as you may find yourself put on the spot, especially if you're live on the radio or TV.

THINGS TO THINK ABOUT

Remember that journalists are not interested in your book, but they are interested in stories, whether they are yours or your clients'.

Have a bank of article topics that you can share with magazines and newspapers that will interest them and their readers.

Be prepared to be interviewed at a drop of a hat, as once you're noticed, you'll be approached by journalists as an expert in your field, and you may well be asked for your comment on topical stories.

Always look for opportunities for publicity, whether it's a book review or a feature in an online magazine.

_____

_____

_____

_____

_____

_____

_____

_____

CHAPTER 15
Stand out on Amazon

One of the secrets to getting your book noticed is by ensuring it is distributed on Amazon, other online bookstores, and in bookshops across the world. You may later have your book published in multiple languages and hopefully you'll reach people who would never have heard of you without your book being published.

In this chapter, I'm focusing on creating an effective sales page on Amazon, as this is the most popular book sales platform. Equally you could apply these tips to other places where you may distribute your book, but love it or hate it, having your book listed with one of the largest internet-based retailers is a great way to promote your book.

Some people think that all they need to do is list their book on Amazon and then wait for the sales to come in, but unless you do some fundamental things first, it won't be that easy.

There are simple strategies you can follow that will help you to get your book up the bestseller list organically and get it found by your ideal readers on Amazon. You'll also find that some of these strategies can be carried out alongside doing an Amazon launch to enhance the reach of your book in chapter 17.

Have the right book title

Choosing the right book title and subtitle that includes the words or phrases that your ideal reader is looking for will help your rankings, and help your ideal reader to find it. If the title does not convey the message in your book and who it's for, then the subtitle will need to be specific. If you're too clever with your words, this might hinder your progress if you're not yet well known. It's also important to note that your title must be accurate as to what your book is about. If your title says something and then the content doesn't meet expectations, then this will cause unhappy readers (go to www.librotas.com/book-title for a blog post that I have written on this topic).

Choose the right categories

It's really important to choose the right categories for your book, as this will help your ideal readers to find you. If in doubt, look at competing books (with high sales) and see which categories they are listed under to help you make your decision.

Pick relevant SEO friendly keywords

In Amazon you have the opportunity to list your book under keywords relevant to your book's content. That's why it's important to get clear about what your ideal reader may search for on Amazon. Just like internet search engines, when you start typing your search term, ideas will pop up in the box. Another way to approach this is to use the Google Keyword Planner tool or FreshKey, the latter of which will show you the popular terms on internet searches and specifically on Amazon.

Hone your book description

Don't just dump your back cover text on your Amazon page without thinking it through! What you put in the book's description box will also help or hinder your book's success. I was recently contacted by someone who had published her book, but was struggling to get sales. As she (at the time) only had three lines of text in this area, this was one of the things that I suggested she change.

In your description, not only do you want to give people a clear idea of what your book is about, but you also want to grab their attention with your hook, and include phrases that will help your book to be found. You may also choose to include testimonials and reviews that are in your book, as this provides good social proof before your new readers leave reviews on Amazon themselves.

Have a well-designed front cover

They say people don't judge a book by its cover, but I don't agree when we're referring to actual books! Although this is something that you should have thought about before now, I want to mention it here anyway. The thumbnail of your book's front cover will appear on your Amazon listing, so make sure that it looks professional and translates well into a small picture. Too much information or a complicated image won't help it to get noticed for the right reasons.

Your book cover doesn't have to be intricate or expensive. You may find that text is all you need to get it noticed — if it's the right text! I talk about creating a great book cover in more detail in *Your Book is the Hook* (www.yourbookisthehook.com).

Get lots of excellent Amazon reviews

If you've seen me beg for reviews for my books, it's because I know how important this is for your Amazon rankings! It may well influence the buying decisions of potential purchasers, especially if people you don't actually know are leaving you (ideally) excellent feedback with five star rankings. But even if your reviews aren't all five star, it shows that people are reading your book, and everyone is entitled to their own opinion about what they read. Just don't respond if you don't agree, as it won't enhance your reputation if you get into an argument with your reviewers.

Your reviews will also impact on Amazon's algorithms to get it found. The more reviews and sales you have, the more likely your book will show in the 'Customers who bought this item also bought' when people are searching for something similar to your book. However, it's important that these are genuine reviews from people who have actually read your book.

Develop your Amazon author page

Did you know that you can have an Amazon author profile? If you've got a book listed already and you don't yet have a profile, do it now – you can do it through the Author Central section. This is a great place to link to your books, detail your biography so that people can get to know you, and include photos, videos, events and what's coming up soon. And it's free! You can also view your books, sales rankings and reviews at a glance.

Be aware that if your book is available on different Amazon sites, for example on Amazon.com and Amazon.co.uk, you will need to create a different author profile on each site.

Use the Look Inside™ function

Also in the Author Central section is the Look Inside™ (also known as Search Inside™) function. If you enable this function, it gives people the chance to browse through your book to sample it, and see whether it's the right book for them before buying it. Usually your reader can view the first 20 pages, so they can quickly decide whether it is the right book for them. On the positive side for the author, when people search for books, in addition to your title and keywords, Amazon use actual words from inside books to help rank them.

Ensure your book is professionally edited

It's all well and good having a great looking listing for your book, but if your book is peppered with spelling and grammar mistakes or it doesn't flow well, this isn't going help you.

When someone downloads or receives a physical copy of your book, the professionalism will reflect your brand, so it's important to get it right and employ a professional editor and proofreader before you publish, even if you are on a budget. Although I'm not going to go into this now as I talked about it extensively in *Your Book is the Hook*, having a great opening will help, especially if you've enabled the Look Inside™ function.

Have an e-book <u>and</u> a physical book

Although we're in the digital age, I do believe that there is a market for both online and physical books. Amazon's digital book is Kindle, and I suggest you have both this and a physical book. This gives your reader a choice as to which they prefer. If you want a Kindle (e-book) version of your book to be available, you will need to sign up to KDP (Kindle Direct Publishing) and there is also an option to sign up to KDP Select so that people can just 'borrow' your book. I'll touch more on this in chapter 19 and you may wish to have an audio version of your book too.

Price your book realistically

If you've not already set a price for your book, be realistic when doing this. Most physical books in the non-fiction arena sell for somewhere in the region of £9.99–£14.99, and Kindle books tend to be lower as there's less cost involved with the production. Although you might argue that the same knowledge and expertise is involved with writing it, there is a psychology with regards to pricing. There is a stage where the price is a no-brainer and your ideal reader won't give it a second thought before they purchase your book.

Bear in mind that there is a cost involved in selling your book on Amazon. With a print book, typically the costs are around 50–60% of your list price. If you price your book reasonably on Amazon, then you can always have offers or discounts when people buy a copy direct from you when networking, speaking or exhibiting.

When considering pricing, also consider what services you are likely to sell off the back of your book. Getting a small, or no, profit may be worth it if your book generates other income for your business.

Be a reseller for your books

Many publishers will automatically include your book for distribution on Amazon, and if they don't, you can use Amazon Advantage to sell your books. You can also be a reseller for your book, which means you can sell your book if Amazon runs out of copies and potentially offer it at a discount.

Publish more than one book!

Publishing multiple books on Amazon will help you to get found. Many of my clients don't stop at just one book. You could produce a combination of Kindle and physical books, and these will help you to get known in your area of expertise. Once people have bought one of your books, they are more likely to find you and buy the others, thus also helping you to build a community of raving fans.

Tell people your book is for sale

This might be obvious, but it's surprising how many people put their book on Amazon and don't tell anyone about it! Then no wonder it's not found and sales don't result, and business success never happens. I've been contacted by many people who have put their books on Amazon and had no sales, which is one of the reasons why I've written this book.

Hold an Amazon launch

I'm going to go into this in more detail in chapter 17, but thought it worth mentioning briefly here. Launching your book on Amazon using the bestseller plan is a great way to create a buzz for your book.

I hope you've found these strategies useful and do look at how you can apply these to other online stores. Just thinking about the things that I've mentioned will help you to get your book noticed, and help you to promote your book. Remember if you'd like support any step of the way, feel free to email me at karen@librotas.com.

I'll come back to Amazon shortly, but before I go into this, I'd like to talk about holding a physical book launch party first, as you are more likely to do this before your Amazon launch.

THINGS TO THINK ABOUT

There are many strategies you can take to enhance your Amazon profile once your book has been listed. Go through the list and implement them one by one as they all complement each other.

Social proof in the form of Amazon reviews will help your book's ranking, and don't worry if you get a poor review; at least it shows that the reviewer is real!

Like any form of marketing, keeping your Amazon profile and books up to date will enhance your book, even after it's been published.

Become a reseller for your book, even if your publisher also distributes your book, as this will allow people to buy your book directly.

_____

_____

_____

_____

_____

_____

_____

_____

CHAPTER 16
Create a buzz at your book launch party

A great way to create a buzz with your book on a physical and offline level is to hold a book launch party for your book.

When you've spent months – if not longer – working on your book, it's nice to not only celebrate your own work, but also thank those people who are close to you. I'm sure they've been your greatest champions and have had to put up with you during this period!

Although it's not necessarily a budget option, a book launch is also a good way to raise the profile of your book and bring your clients together for the occasion. On a personal note, all of my book launches have paid for themselves many times over with connections and clients that have resulted from building my business profile.

There are many ways to hold a book launch party. I've held a few and also attended some which have been held by my clients. It could be a simple affair, such as a book signing in a bookshop, or something more elaborate, like a party held in a hotel or similar venue. Or, as I explore later in this chapter, an online launch is another option that you could consider instead of, or as well as, a party.

My experiences

In my opinion, having a party is a great way of launching your book. There are various ways of doing this and it's important to consider your plan of action at the outset. I've held four very different book launches to date.

The first one was a free event in a beautiful hotel near me in Hampshire. Over 70 people attended. We included tea and coffee and cupcakes branded with my business logo. As part of the event, we raised money for a charity through a book raffle where other authors donated copies of their books. After the initial networking, my mentor and two of my business friends gave talks, and I then had the chance to tell people about the book. I had a professional photographer, and after the speeches and raffle I did a book signing.

The second book launch was part of a multi-speaker event – the Star Biz conference – that I ran in 2012. The book was just part of this and wasn't a clear launch. If I did this again, I'd make it an important part of the event, as it was overshadowed by the great speakers and our firewalk!

My third and fourth book launches were similar in their approach. These events were low cost events rather than free. For both of these, I had amazing cakes made specially for the occasion, which were talking points. The third was in a hotel with bubbly on arrival and a talk by me, and the fourth was in a local cafe where we included a buffet in the price, and again I gave a talk about my story. The latter launch was videoed, which gave me great material to promote the book and the launch many months after the event. For both I included special gifts as a reminder for guests to take away, and did a book signing.

The purpose of your book launch

Before I get into the logistics of what to include and how to do it, I'd like you to consider the purpose of your book launch and what you want to get from it.

- Is it to thank your clients, family, and friends?

- Is it to celebrate your book and congratulate yourself for a job well done?

- Is it to promote your business and make more sales?

- Or is it a mixture of all three?

Knowing the reasons behind why you're holding your book launch will help you to make some decisions about it, such as your budget, whether you're charging, and what's included, so make a note of the purpose before you move on.

It's not just about launching your book, it's about how you can use this opportunity to tell people about it and get people interested in your work.

At this stage I suggest you write down a list of people you'd like to invite to your party as this will influence some of the other points.

The event venue

I've held and attended book launches at very different venues: a private room in a pub in London, hotels, a cafe, community centres, an art centre, and a private room in a restaurant in Florence. Before you book your venue, think about what sort of experience you'd like to create. You may choose to have a themed venue, and if so, what type of unusual venue may support this theme? For example, a sporting book would be fitting in a sporting environment, and an art book would be well suited to an arts venue. If a theme is involved you might also wish to think about how you can dress the room to reflect this.

Do make sure that your venue is fit for purpose. If you'd like to do a presentation as part of your event, make sure that the room is private and that you can hire the relevant equipment (microphone, PA system or projector) if necessary.

The room needs to be big enough for your guests, probably with space for networking and chairs (and maybe tables) if you're giving a talk as part of the event. If you are photographing or videoing the event, allow space for this and think about the lighting.

Remember to be clear on what you want from the venue. Simple things like the layout of room and space available can make your event less stressful once you're there.

The structure of the event and what's involved

That leads me on to how to structure and time the event. I generally hold my book launch parties in the evening as I believe that more people are likely to be able to attend, but your preferred day and time will probably depend on your readership and what they'd prefer. For example, I spoke at a book launch many years ago which was aimed towards business mums, and it was held at a community centre during the daytime. An evening event would have made it very difficult for this lady's ideal reader to attend.

My advice is to plan your structure in advance. Give yourself time for people to arrive and general networking. If you're giving a talk, plan the time you expect to speak for, and allow some additional time for questions. If you are doing something different like a raffle, then do allow time for this too. And, most importantly, give yourself time for a book signing as well!

Let me give an example. Say you're holding a book launch party from 7–9pm, then you might wish to allow the first 30 minutes for general networking. Then at 7.30pm you may give a 30 minute talk. After this you could allow 15 minutes for questions. At 8.15pm you can hold a book signing where people can approach you to buy your book. You could close at 8.45pm and thank your guests for coming. Consider having a buffer in your timescales too. For my fourth book launch, we had to leave the venue by a certain time, and the guests were having so much fun, it was hard to get everyone to leave!

If you are giving a talk, think about the message that people would like to hear from you. Personally I like to hear the story behind why the book was written, an extract from the book, or some of the tips that are included. This is a great opportunity to showcase your expertise, so do take advantage of it. You may also choose to thank those who have supported you through the process or anyone who has contributed their time or stories.

You may also choose to have guest speakers, but if you do this, they need to be talking about you and your journey. Remember you are the star of the event! It is all about you and your book, not someone else's. This is a great opportunity for someone else to be singing your praises, a good thing to do if you're not great at doing it yourself. At the very least have someone you know (an MC – Master of Ceremonies) to introduce you to your audience.

Your budget

The choice of whether to charge or not for a book launch is up to you. There are pros and cons to both. Hiring a venue and including refreshments can be expensive, but if the benefits outweigh the costs, for example you're upselling to a paid-for programme, you're using it as an opportunity to get more business, or you simply want to thank your friends and colleagues, then it's worth considering this. These days I generally charge a small fee towards costs as this does get the commitment of your attendees, although this tends to solely cover the fees involved in putting on the event.

Also consider what's included in the ticket. As you can see from my experiences, there are many things you can include. If you are holding your event in a licensed establishment, having a cash bar is beneficial, but you may wish to include soft drinks, tea or coffee on arrival. If it's an evening event and people may be coming straight from work, then having a buffet, light snacks or canapés is something to consider.

How to sell tickets for the event and why people should attend

Even if you're holding a free event, you still need to 'sell' tickets. From a numbers point of view you need to know how many people to expect, especially if you're providing food or drink.

Like any event, you need to promote it to your prospective attendees and tell people that it's happening. Once you know the date, why not send a 'save the date' email or postcard, just like in advance of a wedding! That way the date will be in your guests' diaries way in advance. Do give yourself plenty of time to plan for it.

When you need to confirm numbers for the event, it will be easier if you have a record of those due to attend. I use an events management system, such as Eventbrite, to invite people and confirm numbers. You can use this whether you are having a free or paid-for event. If you're having a paid-for event, be aware that there is a fee for using this type of system, although I believe it's worth it in return for the other functionalities it gives you, like a guest list and a means to easily contact those who have booked.

Be clear on why people should attend the event. What's in it for them? Although I'm sure that many people will be there because they're interested in you and want to find out more about your book, some people will need more persuasion.

Think about how you can attract new people to your event. Employ social media, share in networking groups, and ask your friends to tell people about it – or you could do a press release for your local paper. Word of mouth advertising is a great way to attract new people.

Create the wow factor

An effective event is one that's run well. My virtual assistant has been in charge of organising each of my book launch parties and does a great job. This means that all I need to do is show up and shine!

If you want to create the wow factor, don't try and do everything yourself. Assign roles to friends and family. Make sure that someone is welcoming your guests when they arrive. You may assign another person to look after you and make sure you're in the right place at the right time, and another to take money for book sales.

Think about how you can create the wow factor at the venue. You might want to dress up the room, and for specific books, having something unusual like a photo booth or other accessories may work well with your theme. But even a simple touch like a pull-up banner with your business details, book and name on it brings together your business and your book.

CASE STUDY
Sheryl Andrews
author of *Manage your Critic – From Overwhelm to Clarity in 7 Steps*

When Sheryl Andrews held her book launch, she added the wow factor. One of her colleagues designed the room for her to make it stand out. She created an amazing showcase for her books, which Sheryl had also used at an exhibition a few days earlier. She dressed the tables and turned the community centre into a book themed venue that wowed! You can see photographs and get the full details at www.librotas.com/free.

When I hold a book launch, I like to do something a little unusual. For my last two parties, I've had fabulous cakes designed and made especially for the events. Although these haven't been cheap, the PR from this alone has given the event a talking point.

I also like to include a little gift to attendees. This might be as simple as branded chocolate, a bookmark, or something else relevant to your book and business. Or you might offer a goody bag that complements your book. What you choose to offer will depend on you and your budget. Ideas and tips are available at www.librotas.com/free.

At my third book launch, Emma Paxton graphically recorded the event. As she'd already provided the illustrations for the book, it brought the two things together. It was a great talking point on the day, and provided me with a souvenir of the event.

At my fourth book launch, winning a book hamper prize was a thrill for one of the attendees, and a great PR opportunity for my author friends who donated their books for the event.

Here are some more client examples.

CASE STUDY
Gina Visram
author of *Happily Ever After for Grown-Ups*

I went to Gina's book launch after firstly helping her to finish writing her book, and later helped her with its promotion. She chose a lovely room in a central London pub and it was packed out with well-wishers. Like many of my clients, she had bubbly on arrival, did a talk, and also had a book signing at the event. She used the occasion to thank everyone who'd been part of her journey – and to promote her book!

CASE STUDY
Louise Evans
author of *5 Chairs, 5 Choices*

When I was editing this book, Louise launched her book *5 Chairs, 5 Choices*. A successful coach and trainer, she lives in Florence, Italy, and works with corporate leaders in global organisations.

I enjoyed travelling to Florence for her book launch party, which she held in a private room in a beautiful scenic restaurant with bubbly on arrival. She used the opportunity to thank those who had been part of her journey, and as it was just before her first TEDx Talk (which I mention later), she used the opportunity to share her presentation with the audience, and read excerpts from her book. She also had a jazz band

and entertained us with a song. She then did a book signing before there was more wine, canapés and networking to finish!

How to use the book launch to grow your business

Like any event, having a book launch party can help you to get great PR and raise your profile. If you can get sponsorship, a newspaper or radio station to cover the event, or use it as a photo or video opportunity, then do so. Remember if you're looking to get press coverage, journalists are more interested in your story rather than the book itself.

Before my first book launch party, I was interviewed on local TV prior to the event. I made the most of the opportunity at the launch of my fourth book to have it videoed and turned the clips into YouTube videos to promote my business and my book.

At the event itself, make sure that people can purchase your book, or if you're charging for the event, allow people to get a copy as part of the ticket price, perhaps offering a discount on the full price.

Having a book signing is a good incentive too, and it's easier for you if you have this prepared in advance. Just make sure that you have enough change and a safe place to store money, and you may consider having a credit card machine to take payment (you can use a computer or smartphone linked to PayPal or a handheld device like WorldPay Zinc or another online provider). You might also offer a discount if people buy multiple copies.

If you're having the book signing live on the day, it goes without saying that you need to have books (and enough of them!). You may think this is obvious, but for one of my book launches, I hadn't actually seen the proof copy ten days before my book launch party. This was a little hairy but luckily we pulled it out of the bag in advance of the big day!

Have a nicely decorated table, a comfortable chair, a nice pen, and think about what you'd like to scribe in the book. In advance of your party, you should do a practice run or two, so that you know where in the book you are going to sign. If you have already received pre-orders for your book, you may wish to sign these before your launch event, as this will save you time.

Don't miss out on other opportunities at your book launch. How can you help people further? If you're going to be offering programmes, workshops or events which will build on the content in the book, why not promote these at the event? Having a special offer or an incentive to book to attend an event may be a pull for your guests.

Lastly, remember to follow up with your guests after the event, and ask people to review your book on Amazon and on social media. Your book's launch starts but doesn't end with your party. Ask people to share their photos of your event online and you could even have a competition for people who have bought your book, like the most unusual place your book has travelled to.

Remember to continue to use the momentum of your book launch. Share quotes from what people have said about your book, share photographs or videos, and remind people how they can get hold of your book.

If you don't have the time or money to hold a physical event, go virtual. You can have an online book launch instead via webinar or hold this as well as a physical launch. This has the added advantage that you can reach people all around the world.

PLANNING YOUR BOOK LAUNCH

Here are some things to think about:

What is the purpose of your book launch party?

_____

Where are you planning to hold your event?

_____

What is your proposed structure for the launch?

_____

What is your budget and what's included in the ticket?

_____

How are you going to sell tickets for the event and why should people attend?

_____

How can you bring in the wow factor?

_____

How will you use the book launch to grow your business?

_____

 **THINGS TO THINK ABOUT**

Know why you're having your book launch and what you want to get from it. If you write multiple books, you don't have to have multiple book launches, but they are a great way to thank people and raise your books' profile.

Leave enough time from the publication of your book until the book launch. You don't have to hold it immediately. There's nothing worse than worrying whether you're going to have any books!

Bring in the wow factor. There are many low cost ways to surprise your guests and help them to remember it forever.

Videoing or photographing the event professionally can provide you with great material. You can view the video from my fourth book launch at www.librotas.com/free.

_____

_____

_____

_____

_____

_____

_____

CHAPTER 17
Become an Amazon bestseller

When I asked you about your goal for your book in chapter 1, did it involve having a bestselling book? I'm sure that you've realised by now that being a bestseller is something that very few people achieve, and actually if you're writing a niche business book, then there are better ways to get a return on your time and investment. Of course it's great to be able to say that you've written a bestselling book, but to get onto the *Times* bestseller list or equivalent, you need a lot of luck, a huge community and a great team behind you.

However, if you've followed the advice in my book and by this launch stage you have built your community and have a great support network, then launching your book on Amazon is something I'd recommend. It's an effective way to promote your book on a bigger scale.

The idea of an Amazon launch is to get your book to number one in their charts. Although in reality there are other things that this type of book launch will do for your business. It will raise the profile of you and your book and, when done well, will help it to get noticed.

There are many people who have written about holding an Amazon launch, and you can make it as complex or as simple as you like. This is the simple version, which I've adapted from the people I've learnt this strategy from.

This is the strategy that I used to get my first and second books to number one on Amazon, and it also worked when I promoted my third as a Kindle book. My biggest success was my first Amazon launch, for *The Secrets of Successful Coaches*, and I'll tell you why in a moment.

These are the steps you need to take to launch your book on Amazon.

1.   Decide your launch date.
2.   Create an offer.
3.   Ask other people to help you.
4.   Get ready for your launch.
5.   Help your helpers.
6.   Promote it yourself.
7.   Measure your success and follow up.

1. Decide your launch date

Usually the date for an Amazon launch will be after or instead of your physical book launch party. You need to give yourself time to set it up, get helpers on board, and get some reviews online. If your book has a particular niche, then you may choose a date that is relevant to this niche, or you may choose to pluck a date out of the air a few months after your book has been published.

The main reason for this longer lead time is because many of your helpers may have planned their marketing in advance and if you want some big names in your industry to help you, then you need to give them time. Besides, if you've been writing your book for a while, giving yourself a breather wouldn't hurt either whilst you promote your book in other ways.

The idea behind having a specific launch date is that the Amazon bestseller plan works when lots of people buy your book on one specific day. The volume of books bought in a short period of time will help to propel it to the top of the charts. You'll probably choose a weekday, although this does depend on your book and your audience, and when they're most likely to be online.

Decide which day you wish to launch your book and designate this as your launch day.

2. Create an offer

To ensure that as many people as possible buy your book on your launch day, I suggest you offer specific bonuses only valid on this date. Your offer will usually complement your book and may include elements such as a webinar, a complimentary call for the first x number of people who buy your book, or another product that supports your launch. Usually these will be something that costs your time rather than having a physical cost.

If you're looking for the complex version, I've also seen people adapt this process by having other business owners offer their products too. But this can make the offer overwhelming and difficult to manage, and it also takes the attention off the star of the show, aka you!

3. Ask other people to help you

For each of my online launches, I've asked other people to help me to reach more people on my launch date. I've put together a list of people who offer complementary services or products and contacted them to help me. For my first book, as I'd interviewed many coaches for the book, most were willing to send the information to their list and share on social media. This was one of the secrets behind my success when I promoted this book. You'll want a long list of people, ideally with a strong community of people who are likely to be your ideal readers. My list of helpers for my first book was pretty long – 50–100 people from recollection – which supported the launch of my book.

The best way to get your helpers on board is to create a standard email and personally send it to them. This email needs to tell people what you're doing, give a brief synopsis of your book, your plan for the launch and the date, and also a request for them to reply.

With my first book, I directed my helpers to a page on my website that had a sign-up box to make it easy for people to say 'yes' to helping me. So that I could anticipate the number of people they could reach, I asked them to share the number of people on their list and it had tick boxes so that they could indicate how they were willing to share my launch, i.e. via their newsletter, Twitter, Facebook and/or LinkedIn. This helped to measure its success.

4. Get ready for your launch

For the day of your launch, you'll need a one page webpage specifically for it. This will include details about your book, why people need to buy it, any supporting offers, and ultimately this is the sales page to encourage people to buy your book on this day.

Make sure that you include a link to your Amazon page and a way for people to get a copy of the bonuses. Ideally have a sign-up box where your new reader has to leave their name, email address, and Amazon order number. They can then automatically join your mailing list so that you can follow up with them.

5. Help your helpers!

When I carried out my online launches, after getting support, I created a list of everyone who had said yes and then I made it easy for them to promote me. I designed emails for them to send out to their communities. I wrote Facebook and Twitter updates so that they could easily share the information that I wanted them to share. I also gave them the choice to amend these materials to suit their audience, which was especially applicable for the standard email. I asked them to direct their followers to the page I mentioned in the point above.

I reminded my helpers the day before the launch and on the launch day itself, and also thanked them for their help afterwards. Don't assume that they'll remember without a gentle reminder or more!

6. Promote it yourself

As well as asking your helpers to promote your offer, it is also essential that you do it yourself through your newsletter, social media and any other opportunities you have during this day. These may include forums, other communities, LinkedIn groups and the like.

You could run a series of targeted Facebook or Google advertisements alongside this. You could also engage in relevant online conversations or physical conversations.

On the day of my second book launch, I was at a networking breakfast. It was a great incentive to start promoting it early and have a multi-pronged approach to getting it noticed.

7. Measure your success and follow up

Ideally keep the day of your launch free. This means that you can correct any problems if they arise and measure your success. Taking screenshots of your progress on Amazon as the day progresses means that you can compare your ranking at different times of the day.

You ideally need autoresponders to follow up with new readers who buy your book. When I did this for my first book, I included the bonuses and also a follow-up sequence to tell my readers how else I could help them. It's also important to later remind your new readers to leave an Amazon review.

This plan will help you get your book noticed. It is not designed as a long term strategy to keep you at the top of Amazon or get you onto any of the other bestseller lists, as this only works with a more comprehensive marketing plan in conjunction with this process. In reality, depending on your niche and your category, you don't need to sell hundreds or thousands of books to reach number one on Amazon. But the most important thing about doing a launch like this is that it is designed to help you to reach more people than you can do alone, and help you to reach those people who may otherwise not hear about you and your great work! It is also allows you to say in your publicity that your book was an Amazon bestseller!

 **THINGS TO THINK ABOUT**

The Amazon bestseller plan is just part of your launch strategy, and it is a great way to create a buzz with your book and reach more people.

It works best when you designate a specific launch date when you promote your book.

You'll achieve the greatest success when you get helpers on board in complementary fields who will help you with your promotion.

You need to help your helpers by giving them the emails and social media updates that they can share with their audience.

_____

_____

_____

_____

_____

_____

_____

_____

CHAPTER 18
Additional book launch tips

It's important to mention in this section that there are other things you can do to launch your book. While they are important the strategies don't each warrant an individual chapter.

Have your book available on all platforms

Although Amazon is the key platform, making sure that your book is available via other means is important, such as Waterstones, WHSmith and Barnes and Noble. There are various tools available to help you to do this. One of these is Nielsen Books, the organisation that supplies the ISBNs (International Standard Book Number) for books. But they do so much more than this. My book designer Sam Pearce provides her advice.

 HOW NIELSEN BOOKS CAN HELP YOU TO ENHANCE YOUR BOOK DISTRIBUTION BY SAMANTHA PEARCE

Nielsen Books are a vital resource for publishers and self-published authors in the UK. They are a leading provider of search, discovery, consumer research, and retail sales analysis tools globally. However more importantly, Nielsen's is the registration agency for ISBN and SAN (Standard Address Numbers) for the UK, Ireland and all Overseas British Territories. They are responsible for:

- Allocating ISBN Publisher Prefixes to eligible publishers and self-published authors.

- Advising publishers on the correct and proper implementation of the ISBN system.

- Encouraging and promoting the use of the Bookland EAN bar code format (this is the standard EAN-13 barcode with an additional 5 digit add-on supplemental code which contains the suggested retail price).

- Promoting the importance of ISBN numbers in the proper listing of titles with bibliographic agencies.

- Providing technical advice and assistance to publishers, self-published authors, and the wider book trade on all aspects of ISBN usage.

UK ISBN Agency

Registering with Nielsen's as a publisher or self-published author is very straightforward, however should not be done until you are nearly ready to publish your first book. This is done so late in the publishing process because part of the application involves the submission of finished title and verso (copyright) page artwork from your book exactly how it will appear once printed, complete with all publisher details. This is to ensure you meet the required standards as a publisher. Once your registration is complete you will be allocated a publisher prefix that will form part of the ISBN number for every book you publish. You will then be added to the Publishers' International ISBN Directory (a printed directory of more than 1 million publishers' ISBN prefixes from 221 countries and territories published by De Gruyter Saur) and the Nielsen book publishers' database (www.nielsenbookdata.co.uk) as a matter of public record.

Your publisher prefix then entitles you to purchase ISBN numbers. As of 2016, Nielsen began to sell ISBN numbers individually, but it is recommended to purchase ISBN numbers in blocks of at least 10. Not only is it more cost effective (£89 for 1 vs. £149 for 10), but also you will require a separate ISBN number for each format of your book. For example, if you plan to release your book as a paperback and an e-book you will require two different ISBN numbers.

More information on registering with Nielsen's as a publisher can be found at www.isbn.nielsenbook.co.uk, and once you have been allocated your publisher prefix you can purchase ISBN numbers online at www.nielsenisbnstore.com.

Please note that if you are using a third party publisher such as Createspace, you will not need to purchase a separate ISBN, although this ISBN is not transferable should you later change publishers. In addition, you do not need an ISBN if you are solely publishing an e-book on Amazon.

Nielsen Publisher Services

In addition to the allocation and regulation of ISBN numbers, Nielsen's offer a number of additional services to publishers and self-published authors:

Book2Look (www.nielsenisbnstore.com/Home/Book2Look) is a digital marketing tool to your book allowing you to market your book more effectively online. Similar to Amazon's 'Look InsideTM' feature, Book2Look provides your audience with a streamlined presentation of your book with readable excerpts, metadata, reviews, audio and video trailers, and links to preferred retailers. Once a widget is created, it can be posted on a website and fans can share it on blogs and social media networks while you retain control of the content being shared. All reader interactions with your book's widget are logged so you can monitor performance of how and where your book is being shared and how many views it is getting. Cost for the widget varies between £24–£90 per title depending on how many widgets you reserve at any one time.

Nielsen Title Editor (www.nielsentitleeditor.com) offers a free listing service to all publishers of English language books regardless of location. This service allows you to register basic information about each of your titles, which are then added to the Nielsen Book Database (www.nielsenbookdata.co.uk), a database used by retailers and libraries in over 100 countries including Amazon, Waterstones, Bertrams, Gardners, Blackwell, WHSmith, The British Library, Book Depository, eBay, and more. An enhanced listing is also available for an annual fee of £222 that adds additional rich data to up to 17 title listings including a more detailed description, reviews, author biography, and promotional information.

Nielsen BookScan Online (www.neilsenbookscan.co.uk) is a service which collects and reports retail sales information of books and publications from more than 35,500 bookshops across 10 key countries worldwide. This information can be used during the planning stage of your publishing journey to help you determine what to write, the right price to sell it for, and how many to print. Once you have published your book, you can use the service to better understand the demand for your title by reviewing sales performance, and to help you to ensure the book is available during peak selling periods and reduce wholesale returns.

The entry-level BookScan Online Sales Summaries (BOSS) subscription is a fairly considerable investment at just under £2,500 + VAT per year, however you get the ability to run an unlimited number of reports on any ISBN number or author, returning sales data from 2001 to present. You also receive a weekly digest on the top 50 selling books across 5 main categories – fiction paperback and hardback, non-fiction paperback and hardback, and children's books. Plus you can set up custom reports emailed to you weekly on the sales performance of all of your own titles.

Samantha Pearce, SWATT Books, professional book design for authors and publishers. Find out more at www.swatt-books.co.uk.

Note: All quoted prices are accurate as of January 2017

If you have taken the self-publishing route, only a few options will allow you to reach worldwide distribution in bookstores, although most will help you to reach a worldwide audience online. You may wish to approach your local bookstores to ask them to stock your book and perhaps let you do a book signing event.

Use Goodreads

Goodreads is another good platform where you can host and promote your book, and is – according to their website – "the world's largest site for readers and book recommendations" with over 40 million users, and is now owned by Amazon.

There are various ways to use Goodreads. As a reader it's a good place to talk about what you're reading, leave reviews and connect with authors. As an author, it's a good place to showcase your book. Although a social (not sales) site, when you create an author profile, add your blog and/or videos, and list your book, you will have more access to potential readers in your genre. When you make friends, build relationships, join groups and give recommendations, then you'll reach people who may be interested in your message.

Goodreads also offers a 'giveaway' service for authors, which means that you can give away a certain number of physical copies of your book in return for a review. This is a good way to increase your reach at this early stage, as Goodreads will promote your book to their audience as part of the process. You can also pay to advertise with them.

Hold competitions

Make the most of the launch strategies that you've employed to date. Having a competition to encourage people to share photos of themselves with your book will raise your book's profile, as will reviews shared on social media or other people's blogs.

Create a book trailer

A well-designed book trailer can help you to effectively promote your book. Like a video trailer for a movie, a book trailer is very similar. With a combination of voice-overs, music, animation and live footage, it will provide information on the book and where it can be purchased. This is something that's worth considering, as not many people do it.

Complement your book with interviews

Lastly, you could complement your book launch with relevant interviews. I did this with my first book as I mentioned in chapter 6. These could be interviews with those you've featured in the book or others interviewing you about your book.

That's it for the launch section. Which actions are you going to take? Doing all of these will help you to get your book noticed, but make sure you have the time to do them well.

Now I'll move onto the next section, where I will show you other ways that you can maintain momentum and build your business through your book.

THINGS TO THINK ABOUT

Use every opportunity to promote your book and remember to continue using some of the suggestions I made in the pre-launch section.

Having a consistent message about your book will lead to new opportunities that you may have never expected.

Don't underestimate the power of your existing contacts who can help you to promote your book and get it out to more people.

Take a moment now to review what you've learnt from this section. Which options are you going to choose to create a buzz for your book when you launch it?

_____

_____

_____

_____

_____

_____

_____

_____

SECTION 3
Post-launch promotion

It's important to consider the ongoing marketing and promotion of your book, even after it's been published. If you don't do anything further with it, then it's never going to grow your business. But don't wait too long. Your book will have a shelf life. Depending on the content of your book, the information that you have shared may become out of date in time and although you can print a second edition or add new content later, keeping your motivation going with the promotion now will keep you on track.

It's also important to remember that generating sales and growing your business is something that you need to do throughout the time whilst you're writing your book. Although it's great to get royalties into your bank account, ideally your book will be generating income through other means. That's when you know that your book is successfully helping you to grow your business.

CHAPTER 19
Go digital and audio

When you launch your book, it may be in hard copy at the beginning. Most people have a delivery of boxes of books to their house or office. And it's a very special moment when you see your book for the first time – your masterpiece in print. Having a physical copy of your book is very easy to do these days, even if you have a limited budget, as you can print your book 'on demand', and I believe this is essential if you want to use it to promote your business.

For now, I want to mention other ways to produce your book. Whilst having a print copy is important, people learn and read in very different ways. You can complement your print book with digital and audio versions, and I'll give you tips on these options in this chapter.

Create a digital version of your book

I recommend that you have your book available as a digital book that people can read online. Amazon's Kindle is the most popular platform that most people use, and you can easily link your Amazon physical book to your Kindle book once you've uploaded it.

These days many people have a Kindle or access to the Kindle app on their phone or tablet. This allows them to take your book with them even if they have limited space in their bag and don't want to carry any extra weight. It's also useful if people want to download your book immediately and can't wait for it to be delivered by post.

Although Amazon allows you to upload a Word version or PDF of your book, I'd advise against this if you want to give your reader a good experience, as they will often contain embedded formatting and/or images that don't convert well to ebooks. For less than £200, a good book designer should be able to create an 'ePub' version of your physical book that you can upload to Amazon KDP.

Publishing your book on Amazon Kindle is free and when you price your book, you can decide whether you wish to take royalties at 35% or 70%, depending upon the price of your book. Once you have the completed document, it's simple to upload your book to the website in the Bookshelf section of Amazon KDP. All you need to add are the details about the book – including your title, subtitle, the ISBN of your physical book, your description, keywords and categories – then upload your cover and digital file, and decide the price. This will ensure that your book is available across all Amazon platforms, not just in your own country. You can also set your book up with Amazon KDP Select which allows people to 'borrow' your book, but this means that you can only host your e-book with Amazon to do so.

At the time of writing, Amazon KDP were introducing more features for authors, including pay per click advertising, and the option to convert your Kindle book into paperback. I'm sure that more opportunities will develop too!

There are other online platforms where you can host your e-book, including Kobo, Nook, Smashwords, and Apple iBooks, so don't disregard these other methods to get your book out there!

You can create your e-book at any stage. You might choose to do this before you print a physical copy or you may wish to do this after you publish your physical book. You may also wish to write a smaller book before you publish a more comprehensive book, which I mentioned in chapter 4 in Helen Monaghan's example. Here is another client's story.

CASE STUDY
Gina Visram
author of *Happily Ever After for Grown-Ups*

One of my business clients, Gina Visram, launched her book in 2014 with my support, but at the time she hadn't done a Kindle version of her book. Later she came back to me to get marketing support for her book and use it to increase her visibility.

To create a buzz for her book, with my support, she did an Amazon launch for her Kindle book. She decided to put together an offer to give it away for free over the Valentine's weekend in 2015 (which worked well with her book's content). This helped her to reach number one on Amazon in her category and re-energised the sales of her physical book.

Create an audio version of your book

There are many people who prefer an audiobook that they can listen to on the go, for example via their phone or instead of the radio when they are on a long train or car journey. In our time-poor nation, giving people different options to 'read' your book will make it more accessible for your readers.

There are various ways you can use audio. You may choose to create audio of part of your book or an abridged version of your book that they can get from your website or iTunes that will give people a taster.

You may also choose to do a recording of the whole of your book that people can buy from Audible, which you can upload via the ACX (Audiobook Creation Exchange) platform. ACX is part of Audible, an Amazon subsidiary, and by publishing your audiobook on their platform, it will be distributed through Audible, Amazon and iTunes. You will earn royalties on sales of up to 40%.

You'll also probably find that people who buy your audiobook may also buy your physical book, so this is a great way to increase your sales!

How to record your audiobook

In August 2016, I did a voice-over demo at Igloo Studios near me in Hampshire. In just three takes, we had a good version of my introduction which is now used to promote the book. At the time of writing, I am planning on recording the whole of *Your Book is the Hook* and probably this book, so that it can be available for those who prefer to learn this way. You can listen to the introduction at www.librotas.com/free.

Although there is an inherent cost to record your book in a professional studio, if you want a high quality result, then having a budget for your audio recording is essential.

If you're thinking about recording an audio version of your book, read on for some tips from Dielle Hannah of Igloo Studios.

⬤ FIVE TIPS FOR RECORDING A GOOD VOICE-OVER BY DIELLE HANNAH

Delivering your voice-over well can make your project and cut down on editing time. Here are top tips to ensure your voice-over session goes well.

1. Be familiar with your script

Being sure about what you are saying will help you feel relaxed, and deliver the script fluidly.

2. Enunciate

We know – it's not cool. But speaking clearly, with correct pronunciation ensures that your script will be clear alongside background music or sound effects.

3. Slow down

Most of us think much faster than we speak, and speak much faster than is necessary for a good voice-over. Breathe, stay calm and slow down. Your words per minute will reflect the mood of your project, however the BBC recommend a broadcasting rate of 160–180 words per minute for radio, which can be used as a guide.

4. Modulate

Don't be too shy to be a bit more tuneful than you would be in everyday speech. Explore your natural higher and lower tones and how they suit your script.

5. Speak confidently

Being well prepared as in tip number 1 will help you avoid hesitation, ums and ahs. Own your space, know your project and deliver with confidence.

For more information about recording your audiobook at Igloo Studios, go to www.igloomusic.co.uk.

One final thing to mention in this chapter is that use of your material is not just confined to your book. When you self-publish particularly, you'll retain the intellectual property to your work. This means that you can use the material again and again in products, programmes, webinars and any way in which you'd like to promote your business and your book. And I'm sure you already know my philosophy – repurpose, repurpose and repurpose! More about this next.

THINGS TO THINK ABOUT

Different people like to process information in different ways, which is why I suggest you have digital and audio versions of your book.

This allows you to reach more people than those who may read a physical book, and some may even buy all three!

You don't have to record your whole book in audio format. You could choose to record the first chapter to give people an introduction in the early stages.

Using a professional studio for your audiobook will give you a high quality return, as will asking a book designer to produce a digital version of your book rather than using a PDF.

_____

_____

_____

_____

_____

_____

_____

_____

CHAPTER 20
Produce products and programmes

One of the things that you need to have in place is the next steps for your reader, as I mentioned briefly in chapter 4. This may well be in the form of a product or products that support your book. Although it would be prudent to have these in place before you launch your book, at the very latest, you can develop them now.

There are people who are going to read your book and take action and that's all they need. There are also going to be people who read it and don't take action! There will be many people who want and need additional and ongoing support, and this is where your products and programmes can help them.

In chapter 4 I mentioned creating your sales funnel: products and services that are aimed towards your ideal readers. To remind you, your lead magnet will lead into your book, your book will lead into products and services, and your products and services will lead into your one-to-one offering. You may have all or some of these in place, depending on the nature of your business.

Although it may seem counterintuitive, creating your online programme alongside writing your book will save you time. My experience of writing *Your Book is the Hook* is a great example. I mentioned it briefly earlier.

I created a low cost online programme in the summer of 2014, and sold it through a series of three free 'question and answer' style webinars. Then I created and ran the programme, and wrote the book alongside delivering the webinars. Although it was tough to do this, it had the following outcomes.

- It helped me to write and publish the book quickly. By the end of the programme I'd written 33,000 words, the bulk of the book. The book went from idea to book launch in just six months.

- Although I already had a framework, I was able to develop my content as I created the programme, and received real-time feedback from my clients.

- It allowed me to reach more people who were interested in the programme and also working with me one-to-one.

- The success of the programme generated £16,000 in income in a short period of time through programme sign-ups, new one-to-one and writing retreat clients, and pre-sales of the book. All before I'd published it.

You can download an in-depth case study which tells you more about how I did this at www.librotas.com/case-study.

The thing about writing a book is that you spend so much time writing it, sometimes your income generating activities go on hold – often without you realising it. You may find that all of your available time is spent on finishing your book, and it's a fine line balancing the two; that's why this is a strategy that some of my clients follow.

There are various ways to do it. With this book, my plan is to launch mini online programmes when I publish, as there is simply only so much information that I can share in a book. In the programmes I can go into more detail, share the steps and also share some resources that I've used successfully in my business.

When thinking about running a programme and writing a book, a question that many people ask me is this: What is the difference between the product or programme and the book? In my view, a product is likely to be more bespoke than a book, especially when you include access to you in the form of webinars or an online forum (or both), and you may also choose to add one-to-one support as part of your package.

How to develop your product or programme

The best way to create your product or programme is to mirror the content that's in your book. You may choose to take part of your process and go a little deeper or give people an overview of your entire process. I've done both.

Personally, I like to promote all of my online programmes online! Generally I will hold a preview webinar where I'll share great content and then upsell to the programme. I will share the information with my mailing list and on social media. I've also had some success with Facebook advertising.

To promote your product or programme, you'll need a sales page on your website and a way to take payment, very similar to the details that I shared earlier around pre-selling your book. You'll achieve the most success if you talk about the problems that your clients are facing and how you will solve them through your programme. By adding social proof in terms of client testimonials and having a clear call to action, this will help you to promote it to the right people.

Then once you've sold the programme, it's time to deliver it. Let me give you a personal example. Since 2015, I've run the 10,000 Word Summer Book Challenge each August. This is an online programme that encourages authors to write their book, with regular webinars, a Facebook forum and the opportunity to upgrade to get one-to-one support with me. The first time I sold the programme, I created the content alongside delivering it. In 2016, I increased the price and had material that I could use again to run the programme for the second time. This is a product that I will regularly offer to clients, as I know it gets great results, and I love doing it.

Then once you've delivered the programme, you can offer people the next stage if they would like to work with you further, so it's important to tell your clients how they can do this. Also do get their feedback and ideally a testimonial that you can use for future promotions.

Although having a dedicated membership platform for your programme is best to manage your content's privacy, a great budget option is to start off by simply having a password protected hidden page on your website for your paid-for content.

Other things you could do

There are other things you could do in terms of creating products.

- You could create a workbook that your readers can complete alongside reading your book.

- You could develop an online programme with a series of videos or audios that people can work through.

- You could create an information product that is recorded, which takes your readers to the next step. This type of evergreen product will help you to establish regular income. I've done this in my programme 'How to get started with your book in 10 simple steps' which is available at www.librotas.com/get-started.

- You could create a membership club that allows you to regularly support your readers, and gives you a recurring stream of income.

- You could run an event or workshop that supports your book. I run regular Book Marketing events which are a perfect bespoke accompaniment to this book.

- You could also offer your readers one-to-one support where they can work with you personally to achieve the results they are looking for.

I've done all of these in my business, from the initial online product that helps people to get started with their book and the 10,000 word challenge, to planning, writing and book marketing events, a writing retreat in Spain, one-to-one support that helps people to go from an idea to a published and promoted book, and publishing packages. I've also had various membership programmes over the years, which have added value to the support I've provided to my clients.

It's important to have the confidence to charge what you're worth and increase your fees to value what you offer. One of my clients increased her fees after starting to write her book, and she was delighted when people started paying them without question. She also packaged her services rather than offering one-off sessions, which also led to increased income in her business.

One of the things that I do is to add value my programmes. An example of this is the writing retreat in Spain. As well as offering five days in the sun, we top and tail the programme with mentoring before our attendees fly to Spain so that they can get the most from their time, support during the retreat, and follow-up support once they've returned home to keep them on track. You can go to www.writingretreats.co.uk to find out more!

Ultimately having different levels will enable people to tap into your knowledge in different ways; some will prefer group support, while others will prefer to get your one-to-one time.

THINGS TO THINK ABOUT

Think about how you can support your readers after they've read your book.

You can write your book and then create your product after you've published or develop it alongside writing your book.

Recognise the value of what you offer and develop your products and programmes based on what your clients want from you.

Develop the confidence to charge what you're worth and package everything that you do. This will add value and help you to support your clients.

_____

_____

_____

_____

_____

_____

_____

_____

_____

CHAPTER 21
Successful speaking strategies

One of the things that I suggest my clients do is to line up speaking engagements when they launch their book. During the writing time, they may not have the time to actually do this type of marketing, but when they have the book to physically promote and sell, it's a great time to get in front of people. Speaking engagements could also include online telesummits, interviews and podcasts, which I mentioned earlier in the book. Specifically in this chapter, I'll share my strategies to help you to develop, hone and present your message and find the right speaking engagements.

Get clear on your topic and message

Getting clear on your topic is a good starting point and is something you can do alongside writing your book. If you're writing a step-by-step guide, why don't you talk about one part of your system, and then you can allude to the other parts which are in your book? Alternatively you could give an overview of your system and tell people how they can find out more. If your book is memoir in style, use your speaking engagement to tell people about your story and what you've learnt from it.

Once you have a clear idea, creating a speaker profile is a great next step. This is a one page PDF that you can send to those who organise speaking engagements. The speaker profile allows you to bring out the salient points of what you want to cover. I suggest you include the following:

- The title of your talk and your name.

- A summary of what your talk is about and who it is for.

- 3–5 bullet points on what people will get from your talk.

- Any other relevant information about your session.

- A short biography, 2–3 paragraphs about you that demonstrates your expertise (and mentions your book!).

- A professional photograph of you and your book cover (if there is space).

- Relevant reviews from other talks that you've given or from your clients.

For an example speaker profile, go to www.librotas.com/free.

I suggest that you have two or three different speaker profiles that give variety to your presentations and choice to those who engage you, but all relate to the topic in your book.

Get speaking engagements

Then it's time to use your speaker profile to get speaking engagements.

Think about your target reader and client and where you can find them. As I work with many coaches and small business owners, I've spoken extensively in front of coaching groups and networking events where I'm likely to find my ideal reader.

Then once you've found the right groups, contact the person who organises the speakers. Check out their website for the best way of approaching them and then do so in this way.

If you're looking for speaking engagements and are not sure where to start, you could put a post on social media saying that you are looking for speaking engagements. I've done this and it has reaped its rewards, but you need to be clear about what you're looking for so that you're not wasting your time.

Once your book is published, you could send a copy of your book to those running the events, as this is a great way to get their attention and also to showcase your work.

In the early days you may find that you're speaking for free (but may have your travel or refreshment expenses paid), but if you have permission to go armed with your books, do a book signing, and talk about how people can work with you, you should recoup your investment.

I've travelled all around the UK for speaking engagements and that's because I know that they work for me. And it allows me to travel, which is one of my first loves! Personally I've found that speaking allows me to reach my ideal clients and many have resulted in working one-to-one with some wonderful people who have sought my help.

To set yourself up for success, I suggest that you have a page on your website where you:

- List your speaking engagements so that prospective clients and speaker organisers can find you. Make sure these include a link to how people can book to see you.

- Include a video showreel of you speaking so that people can see you in action.

- Include some professional photographs of you speaking, which will help to bring your page alive.

- Add some testimonials of what people have said about your speaking and events.

Remember that when you are speaking, it's not about just producing a good talk, although that's part of it, but I'm sure you'd love to generate business from your speaking engagement.

- Do get permission to promote your books; you may also choose to do a special deal on the day. You may also be able to mention or sell other products or programmes too.

- Give people an incentive to give you their contact details and permission to add them to your mailing list, and then you can keep in touch with them after the event. You may also wish to connect with those attending on social media.

- Demonstrate through stories how you work with your clients and the results they've got from working with you.

You may prefer to seek paid speaking engagements, but this may restrict your promotional activities. For a fee, you could join a speaker bureau if you're looking for keynote speeches or high profile paid speaking engagements, as they will seek out suitable opportunities on your behalf.

How to structure and deliver your talk

Although this is not a book about giving talks – and there are a few people who I'd recommend can help you in this area – there are some things that I suggest you consider. As with any form of marketing, you want to grab the attention of those listening to you from the outset and by now you should have some great examples of how you can do this.

The 4MAT process that I mentioned in chapter 9 of *Your Book is the Hook* can be applied to planning and delivering your talk. This enables you to engage your audience and reach their different learning needs.

The great thing about preparing talks about your book is that you always have great content. You don't have to reinvent the wheel by coming up with something new to talk about. For each presentation, I'd suggest you have some clear outcomes to keep you on track, allow time for questions, and know what you'd like the audience to do next.

THINGS TO THINK ABOUT

Don't wait until your book is published to get speaking engagements. Get these lined up as soon as you can. Remember that high quality speaking gigs are usually booked up many months in advance.

Create your speaker profile, which sells you and your expertise.

Have a speaker showreel or video on your website which shows you in action.

If your speaking engagement is unpaid make sure that you can promote your services and your books.

_____

_____

_____

_____

_____

_____

_____

_____

CHAPTER 22
Keep your book visible

There are plenty of ways that you can promote your book, even after it has been published, for many months or years. You can continue the strategies that I've covered above by encouraging people to leave reviews on your website and then sharing these on social media, by continuing to speak at events and doing other things to generate sales. In this chapter, I'll also suggest other simple and easy ways you can continue to promote your book.

Take your book with you everywhere

A really simple and free thing that you can do is to take your book with you when you are doing anything related to your business. Yes, you might need a bigger handbag (or a man bag if you're a gent!).

This would specifically include networking events where it's a great prop for your 60 second elevator pitch, trade fairs or exhibitions, meetings with a prospective client or contact, or anywhere you might meet your ideal clients and readers. I also keep a copy in my car (in a ziplock bag so it doesn't get damaged), so there is always a book not too far away if I need it!

Give away your book

If you're using your book as an 'expensive business card' to attract new business, don't be afraid to give it away. Although it might cost you a few pounds every time you do it, if you get one piece of business from giving away your book or help one new person, then it will most definitely be worth it.

You may give a copy of your book to a prospective client, send a copy with an introductory letter to a corporate contact as lumpy mail, or use it to help you get a speaking engagement. You also may pop a copy in the post to a journalist contact, as they may want to review your book before they write about it.

If you'd like to get some brilliant reviews for your book, then it is definitely worth sending copies to people who are influential in your industry, as people will buy your book based on the social proof of what others say. Write a list of people who you'd like to get your book in front of, and then send them a copy with an appropriate covering letter. And, most importantly, follow up!

When I wrote *Your Book is the Hook*, I interviewed Wendy Shand from Tots to Travel. She wrote her book with the sole purpose of giving it away. She uses it as a lead magnet on her website, and it's been a key factor in the successful growth of her business. Other people will launch their book and only charge for the physical cost of packaging and posting it, which is a good way to promote it, get reviews and use it grow your business.

Attend trade fairs, expos or exhibitions

One of the ways to get in front of your ideal clients is to go where they hang out. You might choose to have a stand, sponsor an exhibition, secure a guest speaker spot, or attend as a guest.

If you can, get a copy of the guest list or exhibition list in advance and know who you would like to speak with, and why. Taking copies of your book is something I'd suggest you do too, as well as plenty of business cards. Then remember to follow up.

During the final edits of this book, I was approached by Angela de Souza to attend her Women's Business Club's Maximise Conference and have a stand in her author hub. My books had previously raised my profile so we'd already connected, and I knew it was a worthwhile thing to do. Doing a combination of the things I suggest in this book will work to your advantage.

Get interviews

As a published author, I'm often approached to be interviewed. This may be as part of another book, a podcast interview, a guest blog post, a telesummit, Google Hangout, or a webinar programme. Although most of these opportunities are likely to be unpaid, if they get you in front of your ideal clients, and you're able to talk about your business and your book, then they are opportunities not to be missed.

Having specific topics to talk about will help you to do these with relative ease as you'll be well practised in your talks. It goes without saying that these should be around the topics that you talk about in your book! And if you are able to make an offer to the listeners, then don't miss out on this opportunity. This may be to suggest they sign up for your free download or a product that will help them.

Look for opportunities

Simply look for opportunities everywhere! Your next steps may be doing keynote talks or perhaps a TEDx Talk. You might consider collaborating with other experts and maybe running your own large scale event or programme.

I launched my second book at my own 'Star Biz' conference. I had seven other amazing speakers and we did a firewalk at the event, which certainly made it memorable.

Here are two client examples of how their books have led to new opportunities.

CASE STUDY
Louise Evans
author of *5 Chairs, 5 Choices*

I mentioned Louise in section 2. As a corporate trainer, one of the biggest differences that writing her book has made to her business is that most of her work over the last year has been around her 5 Chairs system. This unique system is the basis of her book, her training, and the work she does with her clients.

By writing her book, she has developed her knowledge through further research, working with more clients, developing real-life case studies for the book, and putting her expertise down on paper. The book development has helped her to get clearer on her product, the core process, and it's now leading to other projects and possibilities including films, videos and courses.

Telling people she's writing her book has led to some amazing work opportunities. She was approached to speak at a TEDx Talk in Genoa, and following a training session for an organisation, the HR Director asked to pre-order 200 copies of her new book for their managers. And that was before she'd finished it!

Before publishing her book she told me: "Writing a book forces you to market yourself and talk about it more. You have to be able to have conversations with people which have to be convincing and when you're talking about it, you don't realise that you're actually promoting yourself. This has led to new ideas, new offers and new business. Having a book gives you more clout and adds credibility to my courses. People prick their ears up and many people have already been asking me when my book will be out!"

CASE STUDY
Fiona Chapman
author of *The ChapWell Method: The 7 Keys to Your Success, Happiness and Wellbeing*

Fiona launched her first book in 2015, and I recently asked her what her main successes have been since she published it. She answered my questions:

What have been the business benefits of writing your book so far?

"The book has given me a much stronger platform to sell my business and work. People are very impressed there is a book and are able to have a preview of what I am about and also to get to know me. It inspires confidence in my work and what I do, people take a second look, and it gives a good talking point. It provides loads of blog and social media material."

What successes can you share with the readers to inspire them to write and publish their books?

"I have been invited to the Wimborne Literary Festival as an author and the book has been used as a course book by another trainer. It has just put me in another commercial bracket, and attracted more clients. It importantly gave me the sense of purpose to pack up the day job and do what I love, led me onto further study, and built my confidence in what I have to offer!"

Facebook advertising and Google AdWords

Promoting your book via Facebook or Google AdWords is something that you may choose to do, and I touched on this in chapter 9. The reason I'm mentioning it here is that it may well be an important part of your ongoing marketing strategy.

Although I sometimes use Facebook advertising to promote events, I'm more likely to promote my lead magnet, and then offer my book or low cost programme as a 'trip-wire' to take people on the next stage of the book writing journey. When you have a series of autoresponders (which I mentioned in chapter 4) that then promotes how you work and your book, and it will help you to build your community and reach more clients.

You heard earlier from my friend and colleague, Suzii Fido, who talked about Facebook advertising. Here are her specific tips to use this successfully.

⬤ TOP FIVE TIPS FOR FACEBOOK ADVERTISING BY SUZII FIDO

When considering Facebook advertising for your business, there are five key ingredients to achieve success:

1. Objective
2. Image
3. Wording
4. Audience
5. Test and measure

Miss any out and you could find yourself throwing good money down the drain! So let's go into each one in a little more detail.

1. Objective

The first thing you need to work out is what your primary objective is. Are you trying to increase brand awareness? Gain likes on your business page? Or create sales for a product/service? The answer to this question will define the design of your ad.

2. Image

We all know that when you are scrolling through the newsfeed and you see an image that grabs your attention, you stop to see what it's all about and that is what you need to do with your adverts. The image doesn't necessarily have to be related to your goal. Brightly coloured images always attract more attention.

3. Wording

Once you have their attention with the image, you need to make them want to take action. Choosing the right wording is essential. Concentrate on one pain factor and one solution you provide. E.g. Worried about losing money on Facebook advertising? Here are five tips to get a great return on investment. You have a limited number of characters so keep it short and sweet. People need to relate to the issue and be grateful that you have the answer and click on your ad to find it.

4. Audience

With hundreds of Facebook demographics available including age, gender, marital status, location, job position and interests to name just a few, you can really laser target your advertising to your ideal customer. Use these wisely to ensure that you are not displaying your ads to people who are not going to be interested in your product/service.

5. Test and measure

When creating your ads, create them with various images and two sets of wording, as different points attract different people, and set the budget at 50% of your desired spend. After three days, use the Ads Manager statistics to see which image is attracting the best results. Pause the other image ads and create new ads with different wording and the winning image, and increase the spend to 100% of your desired daily spend. We do this to give time as performance shifts settle down after the first three days so your maximum spend is not impacted.

Follow these five steps and you will begin reap the results.

Suzii Fido, Marketing with Ethics, www.marketingwithethics.com.

Affiliate programmes and joint ventures

Another thing to consider is having affiliate programmes or joint ventures, which I mentioned briefly earlier in this book. There are many ways in which this can work to the mutual benefit of both parties. Your book may benefit one of your colleagues and vice versa. If you are inviting other people to contribute to your book, then inviting them to share it with their community will have mutual benefits for both of you.

In 2016 I was approached by a contact for a bulk order of my books that she could sell at one of her events. This is a great way to get in front of more people and it benefited both of us.

You may also find that affiliate programmes work. This may not necessarily be for your book, but this would work for programmes and events that lead from your book. In this situation, you would agree a percentage fee with your affiliates. If they promote your event and one of their clients booked through their affiliate link, they'd be paid this percentage as a thank you for their support.

Author hangouts or webinars

Be proactive with the promotion of your book. Don't wait for other people to promote you to get your book out there. At any stage you can run Google Hangouts or webinars. I regularly run webinars that enable me to add great value to my community. Sometimes I may be promoting an event and other times I'm simply building my list and telling people how I can help them further.

With some of my events, where I've had speakers, I've used this as part of my promotion. It's a great way to introduce my speakers to my community, have them promote me to their community, and also to shape the content of the events.

Write articles and do guest blogs

I've already talked about publicity opportunities, but thought it worth reminding you here. Always look for opportunities to share your story, talk about your book, and ultimately share the expertise that you're getting known for through your book. It is a great positioning tool, so use it! Let me give you a great client example.

CASE STUDY
Emma Heptonstall
author of *How To Be A Lady Who Leaves*

Emma started working with me as her business coach in 2014 after meeting me at an event where I was speaking in York. As a divorce coach she honed her niche and decided to work with ladies who were considering leaving their husband. A trained mediator and lawyer, Emma found that she could use her skills to help these ladies with both the emotional and the practical elements of making the decision to move on.

In a very narrow niche, Emma finds she is often approached by journalists. She is a blogger for the *Huffington Post* and *MeMeMe*, regularly writes her own blogs, and is also a guest blogger for other publications. She finds that these strategies, alongside other marketing approaches, help her to reach more people.

You could also write guest blogs for complementary businesses, and when you build up a good reputation, you'll be asked back for more. I regularly contribute to *Business Rocks* magazine and have been invited to do blog posts for other people too.

Think about which companies or individuals you'd like to approach and how your articles and expertise can help them and their readers. Most importantly, make sure that you use each opportunity to get in front of your ideal readers.

If you'd like more publicity that will promote your book, you may also wish to have some photographs taken of you with your book, which I've touched on already. These are a great way to position you as an author and can be used in many different ways!

Do book offers

At any time during your book's publication you can do promotions and offers for your book or other services. Special offers or including your book as a bonus on a programme are all great ways to raise your profile and bring in additional income.

Write your next book

Finally, a great way to continue to get noticed is by writing another book! After writing and publishing my first book, I said never again. Eighteen months later I launched my second, and six years later this latest book has been written.

If it's not too late, think about this from the beginning. You may have a sequence of books that follow a particular theme, like a series of 'How to' guides. Or your books may simply show a sequence of progression.

This is how I did it.

My first book, *The Secrets of Successful Coaches*, was based on interviews, and although I pulled out the key themes that they were telling me, I quickly realised that I needed to share my own wisdom and knowledge. That led to me writing my second book, *How to Stand Out in your Business*, 18 months later. Chapter 11 from that book became the inspired content for *Your Book is the Hook*. And in this book I've taken the sixth step from *Your Book is the Hook*, on marketing, and I've expanded the information to write this one! In the meantime I also wrote and published *The Mouse That Roars*, my personal story charting my journey.

THINGS TO THINK ABOUT

I'm sure that you've got plenty of ideas to continue to promote your book. I'd love to hear about them. Feel free to email karen@librotas.com to tell me what they are.

I hope that the real-life examples from my clients' stories have inspired you to write, publish and promote your book – or books!

You don't have to stop at one book. Many of my clients have plans for two, three or ten books, and actually having more books to your name is a great way not to be a one-hit wonder!

Before you move onto the final chapter, take a moment to note what you've learnt from this section. How are you going to continue to market your book after you've launched it?

_____

_____

_____

_____

_____

_____

CHAPTER 23
Create your book marketing plan

Your book is the hook that will get you noticed, but its ongoing promotion and marketing is the thing that will help you to increase its longevity. At the end of each section I've suggested that you note down which of the suggestions you are going to use at each stage, so now it's time to take action if you haven't already done so.

One of my clients who was one of the lucky few to review this book said to me: "I've read your book and have got lots of ideas, but how do I choose the ones that are best for me and my business?"

In reality, most business authors can apply many or all of these strategies to market their book. The actions that you choose to take will depend on your type of business, the ideal reader you wish to attract, and where you know you can reach them. Your next steps will also depend on how you prefer to market your business at the moment. For example, you may choose a different approach depending on whether you're an introvert or extrovert – but that doesn't mean that you should stay in your comfort zone! The actions you take will also depend on how established your business is already and how many clients and connections you have who will support you.

I would, however, like to give you some examples that may help you to create your successful book marketing plan.

Scenario 1

If you are a trainer using your book to tap into the corporate market, you'll probably be using tools like LinkedIn during the pre-launch stage. You may well be blogging or using the LinkedIn blogging platform to reach your ideal readers. Getting articles in relevant trade magazines will also help you to build your profile. Depending on your industry, Facebook advertising may help you to target those with particular likes, and you can also retweet and follow your ideal client companies on Twitter.

I'd suggest that you work with the partners you already have in industry and find out who they can introduce you to, and once you've got copies of your book you can send copies to those you want to reach with your message. Also remember that people know people. If you go to networking events, ask for connections with those in your target market, and look at speaking opportunities at trade fairs, exhibitions or for professional organisations.

Scenario 2

If you are a financial advisor using your book to demonstrate your authority with new and existing clients, you may take a different approach. If you're already blogging, this is a great way to showcase your knowledge. You may guest blog and use social media in conjunction with this. Choosing to do video marketing will be a great addition to your book marketing, especially if you answer your clients' specific questions in the videos.

One of the best ways to launch your book is to have a party with your current clients, ask them to invite others who may be interested, and give your book away for free. You may also wish to offer complimentary consultations to those who attend if you have a good success rate of turning these conversations into raving fans or clients. Running informational events and getting the local press involved with your story are other good ways to promote your book.

Scenario 3

If you're a business coach using your book to attract more clients in your niche, then there are many options available to you. Although list building is important for most business owners, I believe it is essential in this instance. Having a strong lead magnet that answers your clients' problems will help you to build your mailing list and a community of people who will want to buy your book. Combining this with developing your social media presence is key, and you may choose to add podcasts or videos once your online presence has been established.

At the launch stage, if you haven't already pre-sold your book, then doing an Amazon launch is a good strategy, as is having a book launch party with your clients and prospects. Speaking and networking are also good strategies to follow. From a post-launch point of view, having products and programmes you create off the back of your book will be good ways to continue to build your business.

Creating your marketing plan

When it comes to marketing your book, one of the things that I learnt when I wrote *The Secrets of Successful Coaches* was to pick three key ways to market my business and do them well, rather than have a scattergun approach. Then, once you've nailed these three things and you've got the systems in place so that they work seamlessly, like I've done with blogging and email newsletters, you may choose to introduce more strategies so that you have a multi-pronged approach to your marketing, spanning both on and offline techniques, like I mentioned in the introduction.

You are welcome to go to www.librotas.com/free for a downloadable marketing plan outline that you can complete with your ideas and actions.

To chat about the best marketing mix that would suit your business and your book, do drop me a line at karen@librotas.com and we can discuss how you can get the ultimate results from your business building book.

Remember that the success of your book is not just about how many books you sell; your success will also come from how you promote other products and programmes from your book, how you develop and hone your message, and everything else you do next!

Your success will result from the systems you have in place to develop your mailing list and community, connect with new and existing clients, and follow up with prospects. For example, simple things like having a questionnaire for prospective clients to fill out will help you to screen people if you offer a complimentary consultation, and having a diary link will make it easy for people to book time to have a chat with you.

Have a team in place to help you manage your workload and do some of the things that you don't enjoy in your business. They'll also be able to provide you with their expertise and this will support the success of your business and your book. Remember that one of the reasons why you wrote your book is to be an expert, and if you're always doing everything yourself, you'll struggle to be that expert.

So how are you going to get started?

Make a bigger difference

What I love about helping more published authors to be successful is the fact that you can reach more people than you can do with a website, blog and social media presence – they are simply the mechanisms that support your business and your book. And I'm sure that reaching those who need to hear your message is why you came into business in the first place. I know it was mine. But as you have developed your business, you've quickly learnt that you do need to build a sustainable business (and income) to continue to help people. So what else can you do with your book to reach more people and make a bigger impact in the world?

What you now have is a sales tool in your hand. Something that you can promote that allows you to attract more clients who want to work with you, without feeling like you're selling to them. You have a tool that allows you to attract more publicity. It's easier for people to get what you do and how you can help them. Your book is the hook, so go ahead and use it!

NEXT STEPS

You can download additional resources at **www.librotas. com/free** including some of the links and information I've included in this book.

When I finished writing this book, I realised that there was so much more I could include, but I had to stop somewhere. So please do sign up for my free newsletter and blogs at www.librotas.com, so that you can keep up to date with new information and articles that will evolve from writing this book.

Find out more about how I work at www.librotas.com. You can also find out about our online programmes and upcoming events, including the Planning and Writing mini-retreat where we take you through the six-step process to plan, write, publish and market your book, our Book Marketing event where you can put your learning from this book into practice, and the writing retreat where you'll have time to get your book written in a beautiful and tranquil environment. And if you'd like my personal support in any part of the book writing, publishing and promotion process, then do drop me a line.

Please keep in touch and I'd love to know the results that you've got from reading this book and implementing my suggestions. Oh and please do leave a review on Amazon!

You can email me at karen@librotas.com or contact me via my website. I look forward to hearing from you.

Contributors to this book

Steve Bimpson, Think Big – www.justthinkbig.co

Ginny Carter, Marketing Twentyone
– www.marketingtwentyone.co.uk

Alison Colley, Real Employment Law Advice
– www.alisoncolley.co.uk

Mark Edmunds, Shooting Business – www.shootingbusiness.com

Nicky Kriel, Nicky Kriel Social Media – www.nickykriel.com

Suzii Fido, Marketing with Ethics – www.marketingwithethics.com

Louise Craigen, Platform Social – www.platformsocial.co.uk

Naomi Johnson, The Profile Company – www.theprofile.company

Ellen Watts, Ellen Unlimited – www.ellen-unlimited.com

Lisa Ferland, Knocked Up Abroad – www.knockedupabroad.eu

Ebonie Allard, The Entrepreneur Enabler – www.ebonieallard.com

Helen McCusker, Bookollective – www.bookollective.com

Samantha Pearce, Swatt Books – www.swatt-books.co.uk

Dielle Hannah, Igloo Studios – www.igloomusic.co.uk

Case studies

Helen Monaghan, HM Coaching – www.hmcoaching.co.uk

Sheryl Andrews, Step by Step Listening
– www.stepbysteplistening.com

Jenny Phillips, Inspired Nutrition – www.inspirednutrition.co.uk

Rochelle Bugg – www.rochellebugg.com

Louise Wiles, Thriving Abroad – www.thrivingabroad.com

Jeremy Glyn, The Inside Track – www.theinsidetrack.guru

Lorraine Palmer, Uncovered – www.uncoveredltd.com

Gina Visram, Limitless Coaching – www.limitlesscoaching.com

Louise Evans, The 5 Chairs – www.the5chairs.com

Fiona Chapman, The Chapwell Method
– www.chapwellmethod.com

Emma Heptonstall, The Divorce Alchemist
– www.emmaheptonstall.com

About Karen Williams

- Karen Williams is the Book Mentor and specialises in working with coaches, therapists and transformation experts. Her passion is helping them to reach more clients, make more money and do what they love, specifically focusing on helping them to get noticed through writing a book.

- She is a qualified coach, NLP Master Practitioner and firewalk instructor. She is a speaker and the author of five business books, has contributed to many other books, and supported her clients to do the same.

- Karen also loves to do speaking engagements and crazy stuff too, like jumping out of planes and helping people to walk on hot coals!

A dream to change the world

When Karen Williams trained as a coach, she wanted to change the world and soon realised that she could only do so one person at a time. Her passion is working with solopreneurs who want to make a difference. But they also know that to do this, they need to learn the skills to create and grow a successful business, and then have the courage to implement these.

She is known for helping her clients to succeed by standing out from the crowd, getting noticed and being an expert in their business – as well as overcoming the fear that might stop them. Through this she can create a ripple effect, as she gives them the resources, abilities and confidence to transform the lives of their clients and make a bigger difference.

Karen's journey

Karen's journey into business started in January 2006, when, after spending 15 years in the corporate world in human resources and training roles, she realised that she didn't want to do it anymore. She'd heard of this thing called coaching, and employed her first coach to get her career back on track. Not only did she find a new job, but she discovered a vocation that she really wanted to pursue. She trained as a coach and, in November 2006, Self Discovery Coaching was born.

She became a career coach supporting people to find a job they love, but she knew that to be successful herself she needed to do more than just be a great coach. That's why she interviewed and learnt the secrets from more than 25 top performance coaches including Michael Neill, Dawn Breslin and Gladeana McMahon and published her first book based on what she'd learnt in 2011.

This first book was *The Secrets of Successful Coaches*, which became an Amazon bestseller, and her second book, *How to Stand Out in your Business*, was published in 2012, which shares her unique Seven Step Success System.

Since 2010, she has been working with coaches, consultants and therapists in business to teach this learning and help her clients to get great business results, and most recently has concentrated her work on supporting business owners who want to write a business building book.

She published *Your Book is the Hook* in 2015 which takes people through her six-step process to write a book. At the same time she was writing a book about her own journey and published *The Mouse That Roars* in 2016. This, her fifth book, was published in 2017.

Karen's passion is to help more business owners get their book written and help them to use it to grow their business. She is a sought after speaker, and loves running events and her writing retreats. After supporting clients with their books for many years, she rebranded her business as Librotas in January 2016.

She has also been featured on local TV, UK and international radio, in various publications including Psychologies, Marie Claire, Coaching at Work, Rapport magazine, Personnel Today, the Daily Express, and Portsmouth News, and she speaks at events across the UK and abroad.

On a personal note

Karen has also conquered her own challenges. In her book *The Mouse That Roars* she shares some of these stories. This includes the 'Year to Live' project where in 2012 she decided to do things that she had never done before. Although happy with her life, she knew that there were things that she'd love to do.

During that year she decided to go skiing for the first time – after always saying she'd go one day. She also jumped out of a plane for charity (and took three of her clients and husband with her!). She also qualified as a firewalk instructor and has helped dozens of her clients to walk on hot coals, break through boards and walk across a bed of broken glass. But don't let that put you off!

In addition, she signed up to do a charity trek, and in September 2013 she walked the Inca Trail in Peru to Machu Picchu for the

Genesis Research Trust (Women for Women) and was part of a group of 21 ladies who raised over £90,000 for charity. This was a bigger achievement than Karen had imagined as she was hospitalised in Peru just before the trek started, so she was glad to make it! Their fundraising was celebrated at the House of Lords in May 2014 with a presentation by Lord Robert Winston.

Karen knows that through her work, teaching and writing she can support more people, and leave a legacy that will help future generations. And she wants to help you to do the same!

Contact Karen

Find out more about Karen and her work at www.librotas.com and you can email karen@librotas.com.

You can also follow Karen on the following platforms:

Facebook: www.facebook.com/librotas

Twitter: www.twitter.com/librotas

LinkedIn: www.linkedin.com/in/karenwilliamslibrotas

YouTube: www.youtube.com/karenwilliamssdc

Lightning Source UK Ltd.
Milton Keynes UK
UKHW020630150121
377105UK00011B/1209